JUST AN INTRODUCTION

Sweet Teacher Friends,

We are excited to begin this journey through James with you. Before we get too far, there are a few things we would like you to know.

First, allow us to introduce ourselves for those who do not know us.

Bonnie was born and raised in a rural Georgia town. Studying at Southeastern Baptist Theological Seminary brought her to North Carolina. During her time at seminary, she studied Women's Ministry, but God had a slightly different plan for her to teach in a local kindergarten classroom. If you want to get to know Bonnie more, follow her on Instagram: @bonniekathryn

Bethany was born and raised in a small town in Virginia. She studied Communications and Women's Ministry at Liberty University. From 2007-2016, she was living the city life in Florida. In 2016, she moved to North Carolina to teach middle and high school English. Though English is a passion, Bible trumps even her love for grammar...and y'all, that's big! If you want to get to know Bethany more, follow her on Instagram: @theenglishnerd

Secondly, let's talk logistics for a minute.

We will be using the English Standard Version throughout this study. When we ask you questions or provide fill-in-the-blank sections, the ESV will help you best to answer these questions and fill in the blanks. If you do not have an ESV Bible, you can use the online version found at www.esv.org. With that said, you may use any version you choose. You **just** may find that the wording in other versions does not match the wording in our questions.

Grammar baubles...while Bethany LOVES her some grammar, we have also chosen to make our study conversational. So, yes, that means we've started sentences with conjunctions. We've ended sentences with prepositions. We've purposely used fragments in places. Bonnie thinks that's SO okay! Bethany says it's okay because as she tells her students, "If you know the rule and know you're breaking it and have a reason for breaking it, it's permissible." (**Just** don't apply that to life, please 😊)

Lastly, let us share a little bit about our heart behind this study.

One of the main goals of Teachers in the Word is to spur you, a teacher, to be in the Word. While there is a time and place for studies...even like this one...there is also a time and place for sitting down with our Bibles, opening them, and allowing the Holy Spirit to guide us into understanding of His Word. What better time than now to allow Him to help us to do **just** that.

The first time a teacher releases her students to try a task on their own, struggles are expected. It's new. It's different. It's challenging. That's okay. In fact, that's normal! Teachers, hear us: you are the student. You will struggle. You will find some of this material challenging. That's okay! Don't be like some of our students who get frustrated and shut down, never to return. We have one word for you: persevere. As Jen Wilkin has said, Bible study is more like a savings account than a checking account. You don't go into a savings account to get money often like you would a checking account. You go into a savings account to make deposits more than withdrawals. Bible study is a time to make deposits into your mind and heart - deposits of God's truths, so that when those truths are needed, the Holy Spirit can bring them to mind again. When Bible study gets tough...or even when it's confusing or feels empty...keep making the deposit by showing up again and spending time with God's precious Words.

Our prayer is that this study will challenge you to live a **just** life, **just** like James, who lived **just** like Jesus. He really is **#justwhatyouneed**.

Bethany and *Bonnie Kathryn*

JUST BEFORE YOU BEGIN...

As you begin this study of James, we are challenging you to be a Teacher in the Word. We want you to learn to digest Scripture rather than **just** ingest it. Ingesting is simply swallowing whole the information you hear without processing it with your mind. We want you to learn to digest - to ask questions of the information you receive, to meditate on the information you are given. Meditate comes from a Hebrew word that literally means "to chew the cud." Yes...like a cow! The Holy Spirit knows how much we can handle, and when He knows that we are ready to fully digest and understand a portion of Scripture, He will open our eyes to it. In the meantime, our job is to continue reading and studying and meditating on passages of Scripture...yes, even - no, especially - challenging ones. We are to continue making those deposits in our spiritual bank. It is 100% okay to walk away from Scripture with unanswered questions. There is learning IN the struggle. We know that as teachers, which is why a student struggling encourages us. We know they are learning AS they struggle. Struggle. Meditate. Persevere. Deposit. Digest.

Our challenge to you is this: BEFORE you touch the remainder of this study, we want you to read through the book of James on your own. We want you to learn to "...love the Lord your God... with all your **mind**," learning to "chew the cud" even before we guide you through the text.

Now, don't throw a conniption fit, but we want you to read through the 5 chapters of James at least 3-5 times on your own. Yes, 3-5 😊 While reading, we encourage you to ignore where chapters begin and end. (Side Note: The Bible was not originally divided into chapters and verses. Translators added them to break down the ideas and help us locate where information is found.) Read ONLY the amount you can chew for that day...even if that is 1-2 verses. This means that you likely should not be able to read and digest an entire chapter in one sitting.

We encourage you to highlight, underline, circle, annotate in any way the Lord directs you as you read. For those who are a little fearful of that *annotate* word, it simply means to make notes, ask questions, jot down thoughts. We know that writing in your Bible may be new to some of you. If you are totally scared to write in your Bible, we encourage you to print out a copy of the chapters and write on those.

☐ I COMPLETED A READING OF THE BOOK OF JAMES ON _____

☐ I COMPLETED A READING OF THE BOOK OF JAMES ON _____

☐ I COMPLETED A READING OF THE BOOK OF JAMES ON _____

☐ I COMPLETED A READING OF THE BOOK OF JAMES ON _____

☐ I COMPLETED A READING OF THE BOOK OF JAMES ON _____

HOW TO USE QR CODES

We both use QR codes in our classroom. QR codes are a fun way to make learning tech-based and interactive. Bethany uses QR codes for self-check in her centers. It helps her to avoid having 20 questions during an activity since students can self-assess with them. Bonnie uses QR codes for write-the-room activities, listening-to-reading activities, and to show how-to videos for handwriting. She begins the school year teaching her five-year-olds about QR codes and how to use them on the class iPads. We believe that if Bonnie's kindergarten students can use a QR code reader, so can you!

STEP You will want to download a FREE QR code reader app on your iPad, iPhone, or Android phone. Do not pay for one. There are SO many free options that work well. If you find that one is acting quirky, delete it and pick another free option. If you have a newly updated iPhone and/or iPad, open your camera and hold it over the code. The weblink will pop up on your screen. Tap it, and it will take you to the site. No app necessary!

STEP Open your newly downloaded QR code reader app. You will need to give it access to your camera. It will prompt you.

STEP The app will have a square box that you will hold over the QR code. It should scan immediately, and it will take you to whatever the QR code is linked. Essentially, the QR links to different webpages. Throughout this study, our QR codes are linked to videos.

STEP Try it out here:

Disclaimer: We do not own the rights to any outside links that are included. The QR codes and bit.ly links are simply to be used as a resource and are considered bonus material, not main content. Because we do not own them, we have no control over what the original owner does with the link. If a link or QR code becomes inactive, we are unable to fix this issue. You can search the song title and/or artist and find a similar version.

JUST JAMES ▷ JUST DO IT CHALLENGES

We have created weekly social media challenges for you so we can interact on social media. Please share your challenge pictures in our Teachers in the Word Facebook group or on Instagram using the hashtags **#justjames** and **#teachersintheword**. Please remember that in order for us to see each other's posts on Instagram, you will need a public account. We will periodically share your posts on our main Teachers in the Word Instagram and Facebook page. These challenges are meant to be for fun and are ways to practice being "doers of the word," not **just** hearers of the Word. They are certainly not meant to draw attention to ourselves, but rather to spread the love of Jesus to those around us (Matthew 6:1).

1 Choose a teacher friend and help them complete a school related prep activity: laminating, cutting out things, a classroom decor project, making copies, grading papers, etc.

2 Pack a book bag for a student that is in need of school supplies and drop it off at a local ministry that collects backpacks or keep it in your classroom for a student that might need it the current school year or the coming school year.

3 Create welcome packets for new or visiting students that might encourage them in the new and different transition that is taking place in his or her life.

4 Create a stash in your classroom of personal hygiene and food supplies to periodically give to students who are in need. If you are located in an affluent area, have students bring in items so that you may bless another teacher in a less affluent area.

5 Pack small hygiene packs to place inside your car to give to the homeless that you may see on the road. You can include personal hygiene items and small gift cards where they may purchase food.

6 Ask admin if there is a project at your school that you could complete to help relieve a burden from his or her shoulders: painting a room, cleaning out a closet, setting up a teacher work room, visiting students in need, etc.

Weekly videos can be found at http://bit.ly/JustJamesVideos

WEEK 1

SCRIPTURE MEMORY: Count it all joy, my brothers, when you meet trials of various kinds, for you know that they testing of your faith produces steadfastness. And let steadfastness have its full effect, that you may be perfect and complete, lacking in nothing.
James 1:2-4

While Bible Study looks different for every person and changes with every season of life, we thought it might be helpful to give you a glimpse into our person Bible Study habits. We in no way want you to think that we have it all figured out. We also don't want you to think that you should do exactly what we do. But at the same time, sometimes it's helpful to see what others do so that we can try on their ways for size, so to speak, and discover what *does* work for us.

FROM BONNIE

Bible study habits change for me depending on the day and season. During the weekdays when school is in session, my times are a bit more sporadic and often shorter whereas on the weekends and during summers and breaks, I tend to sit with the Word more...and always with a cup of coffee! **#coffeeislife**

When I study, I like to go through one book at a time. I chew on the passages little by little to get all I can from them. As I read - whether in my Bible or in my Scripture journals that I've recently stumbled upon (booklets that have space for notes...from Amazon) - I mark up the passage. I underline parts that stick out and circle words I need to look up in the dictionary. I write definitions and thoughts beside each verse or section. I also like to utilize apps/websites like Blue Letter Bible to read commentaries and check out the original language (Greek and Hebrew).

FROM BETHANY

My study times also change based on the amount of time I have for the day. Weekends, breaks, and summers are my jam - I love to grab a cup of coffee and sit with the Word for as long as I possibly can. Now, I am an **#englishnerd**, so keep that in mind as I tell you what I do. I, too, sit with one book at a time. I don't tend to jump around because I love context.

I usually begin by reading background information. I have books that give background, but I also use commentaries on apps/websites like Blue Letter Bible and Bible Study Tools. As I study, I mark up my Bible. It sometimes looks like a **#hotmess**, but I like annotating and making connections because both help me to process. I also keep a notebook where I write personal connections or pieces of commentators' thoughts that I want to preserve for later. I enjoy checking out the original language. I also look up cross references, etc. But I ALWAYS sit with the Word on my own before I do anything else. I want to allow the Holy Spirit to guide me first before I start tackling commentaries and Greek and Hebrew.

Nicknames. You either love them or hate them. Bethany comes from a family that never used nicknames. In fact, she hates...with a passion...when people call her "Beth" as though that's her name. ☺ Bonnie, on the other hand, comes from a family that loves them some nicknames. She not only has them herself, but she gives them to others, too, students included. Sometimes nicknames are derived from your name like the people who insist on calling Bethany "Beth." **#justno** Other times, nicknames are derived from your personality like Carleigh Ray. While this little one's middle name is not "Ray," Bonnie has tacked it onto her name because her presence is like a ray of sunshine.

James was obviously the receiver of **#allthenicknames**! Seriously, the man had soooo many nicknames! However, lucky for us, his nicknames were derived from his personality, so by studying his nicknames, we can learn about him as a person.

As any good English teacher would tell you, it is vital that we know about our author before reading his or her works. Writing is always influenced by who we are and where we came from, so before we dive too far into the text of James, we need to get to know James first.

NICKNAME #1

Let's start with the nickname he gives himself in chapter 1 verse 1. Go ahead and read James 1:1 and write below what he calls himself.

```



```

The fact that James doesn't tout his status from the get-go says a lot about his heart. We see his humility from the beginning. We literally get three words into his letter and can unpack a world of knowledge from those three little words. James, while a church leader and a family member of a Very Important Person (more on that in a minute), does not parade his titles, but rather submits himself to God's authority and recognizes that he is only where he is because God sought him out, saved him, and placed him in such a position.

The Greek word for "servant" is *doulos*. It means "one who gives himself up to another's will whose service is used by Christ." This wasn't a word that many would've wanted attached to their name. Many wouldn't choose to nickname themselves something that could also be rendered "slave." Yet, James did. And, in fact, he opened his letter by letting his audience know that he was James, the servant, the *doulos*, the slave, of God.

How many of us would introduce ourselves that way? Usually, we introduce ourselves by attaching the highest title we hold to our names rather than the lowliest, yet James did quite the opposite. Why might he have done that?

```



```

Well, aside from the fact that he was exposing a part of his heart to us - letting us know that he was coming from a place of humility - he most likely wanted his audience to know that despite his titles, he was **just** an ordinary man, choosing to follow God...like them.

NICKNAME #2

Another important nickname, or well, maybe not so much a nickname as a fact...turn to Mark 15:40. Who does it say James's mother is?

That Mary would be Jesus' mother, Mary, as well, making James and Jesus half-brothers. Most commentators (people that study the Bible) agree that he was Jesus' oldest brother. In Mark 15:40, you saw that they called him "James the younger." Younger here, or Less - as some translators render it - is like our "junior." He was the junior of Joseph, the firstborn of Joseph's.

According to John 7:5, even Jesus' brothers didn't believe He was Who He said He was, so to read James's letter that preaches the Gospel of Jesus again shows James's humility. Though he once didn't believe, he eventually humbled himself in belief.

NICKNAME #3

The next nickname of James is rather unique. It gives us a great insight into James's personal life. He was known as "Camel Knees." Yep, you heard us right 😊 Let's have a bit of a history lesson for this one.

An ancient commentator of church history, Eusibius, quoting Hegesippus, (Is your tongue tied yet? 😵) said, "[James]...was in the habit of entering alone into the temple, and was frequently found upon his knees begging forgiveness for the people, so that his knees became hard like those of a camel..."

Do yourself a favor and do what we did...Google "camel knees." We think you need a visual to better paint the picture of this nickname that teaches who James was.

Okay, we must ask: what are your thoughts on those images? This ain't a spiritual question, now. We are **just** curious. Seriously...DM us your thoughts @teachersintheword 😂

James's humility yet again shows itself in another nickname. He was a praying man, and not **just** one known for praying for himself and his own needs, but also for the people around him. What a goal to aspire to be like him in this area! What would happen if we all prayed for those around us, for our country, for our world like James prayed? What if we prayed so much that our knees told a story to those who saw us?

NICKNAME #4

The last nickname we are going to look at for James is perhaps the most impactful simply because it sums up who he was, what he was about, and what he was writing. This nickname fueled the very title of this study: **Just** James came from James, the **Just**.

Why don't we first define the word "**just**." No need for fancy dictionaries. **Just** head to dictionary.com or a similar online dictionary and record the definition below. Be sure to record the definition for the adjective form of this word.

[   ]

James was known for living according to what he believed and what he preached. He wasn't **just** a "hearer of the Word," to borrow his words from James chapter 1, he was also a "doer." **#justjames** was **#jamesthejust** who lived what he preached: a **just** life.

You see, James had every reason to say things like "I'm **just** Jesus' brother" or "I'm **just** a servant," but instead, he humbly submitted his life to Christ and chose to live a **just** life that could be a living demonstration to those around him. His **just** life not only proved to be an example to those in his lifetime, but his life and words are now an example to us as well.

JUST JAMES ▷ ⟩⟩⟩

As teachers, we have a tendency to say things like "I'm **just** a teacher...what can I do?" But, see, really, we are teachers, empowered by God's Spirit, who have the ability to be living demonstrations to those around us: "doers of the Word," "camel's knees" teachers, humble teachers. **Just** like James's legacy lives on, ours, too, can live on. Instead of being **#justateacher**, we can be a **#justteacher**. See what a difference moving that little, tiny, article, a, makes?

Let's ask the Lord to help us to be **#justteachers** in the school year, why don't we? Spend some time in prayer asking the Lord to help you to be a **#justteacher**, who is known for being a "doer" and a "pray-er."

JUST ~~A~~ TEACHER

MY LORD, MY SAVIOR AND JUSTIFIER,

So we know a little more about James, now, but good students of literature don't **just** need to know about the author, they also need to know about the author's audience. Today, we want to take a little trip back in Scripture with you to help you get to know the Twelve Tribes. As Jen Wilkin says, "We can't fully appreciate the sweetness of the New Testament without the savory of the Old Testament" (44). So today is our savory, so that we can get to the dessert of James later.

James writes to the Jews, who knew the Old Testament well. These are the same Jews who were taught to recite Scripture from the Old Testament before their feet hit the ground for the day, before they left their homes, during the day at certain times - they were students of the Word. So, we, too, must be students of those same Words in order to understand where James is coming from.

In order to do that, let's use a timeline to keep all of these events straight.

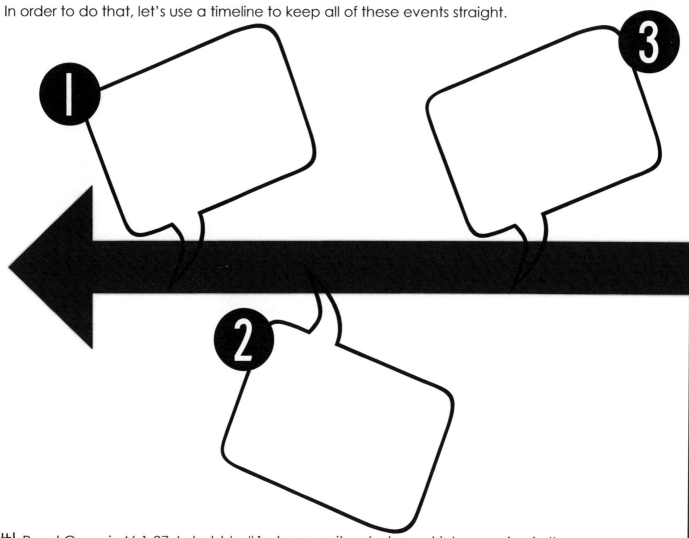

#1 Read Genesis 46:1-27. In bubble #1 above, write what event is happening in these verses.

#2 Turn to Genesis 49:2-27. In bubble #2 above, list the names of the Twelve Tribes of Israel. (Hint: Jacob's sons' names.)

#3 Read Genesis 50:22-26. In bubble #3 above, write what event takes place in these verses.

#4 Read Exodus 1. Verses 1-7 review bubbles 2 & 3. Read verses 8-22. In bubble #4 below, write what event takes place after Joseph's death.

#5 Turn to Exodus 6:1-13. In bubble #5 below, record what God promises to Moses, the Israelites' leader. (Hint: Verse 5 shows specifically what the God promised.)

#6 Turn to Joshua 13:1 and 7. Read those 2 verses, and in bubble #6 below, write what the Lord says to Joshua.

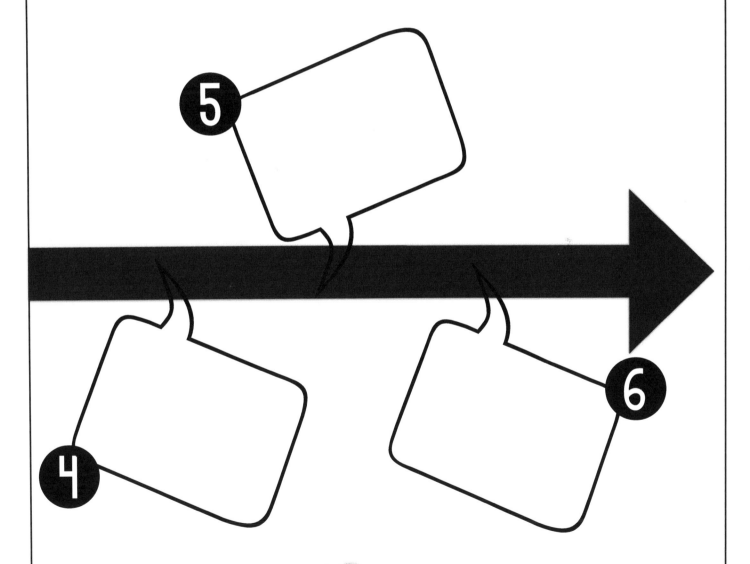

SHEW! IS YOUR BRAIN TIRED?
SO...WHY IS ALL OF THIS INFORMATION IMPORTANT?

In order to understand who someone is, we have to know his or her background. And not even **just** that person's background, but his or her family's background. Whether in a positive way or a negative way, our past affects us. This is true of the Jews as well.

If we had asked you to dive into the book of James without any prior knowledge of who the Jews were or what they had gone through in their past as a race of people, you wouldn't fully grasp why James says what he says to them. His word choice even speaks to them specifically and their past as we are going to see.

LET'S RECAP >>

Jacob moved his family to Egypt as the Lord asked him to do. While in Egypt, the Israelites (the Jews), multiplied greatly.

Before Jacob passed away, he blessed his sons, who were also the namesake of the Twelve Tribes of Israel...the people to whom James is writing.

Joseph, one of Jacob's sons, dies, leaving the Israelites to fall into the hands of Pharaoh.

Pharaoh oppresses the Israelites, refusing to let them go after many requests from Moses.

God speaks to Moses, the Israelites' leader, and tells him that He will not forsake the covenant He made with Abraham, Isaac, and Jacob. He vowed to give them the promised land of Canaan, and He was going to make good on that promise because He is a Faithful God. That's **just** Who He is.

Moses was finally able to rescue the Israelites from Egypt, but due to disobedience and grumbling and complaining, the Lord made the Israelites wander in the wilderness for 40 years.

At the end of their wandering, Moses passed away, and Joshua took up leadership over the Israelites. He led them into the land of Canaan, their Promised Land.

WHILE THIS INFORMATION WILL BE IMPORTANT AS WE STUDY JAMES, THE ENTIRE BIBLE TEACHES US ABOUT GOD AND WHO HE IS. SO LET'S PAUSE AND ASK OURSELVES: WHAT DID WE LEARN ABOUT GOD THROUGH OUR READING TODAY?

DAY 3 ▶▶ SINFULLY SCATTERED

Soooo did you feel like we kinda left you hanging on a cliff yesterday? It's like we toured you through a section of the Old Testament and then **just** abruptly hit the brakes. 😮 We promise there was a reason for that whiplash!

Today, we're going to help you connect the dots because every good teacher knows that if you don't help students connect the dots, the lesson was unsuccessful and unfinished.

Before we get too far, go ahead and re-read James 1:1. According to that verse, where are the Twelve Tribes - or in what condition are the Twelve Tribes? (**#englishnerd** hint: In most translations, it is either a prepositional phrase or an adjective clause that follows immediately after "the twelve tribes.")

Depending on your translation, you may be left asking, "What does that mean?" We would be poor teachers (and Bible tour guides 😊) if we didn't help you define the term. Sooooo…

James is writing to the Twelve Tribes who were no longer living in their homeland. They had been scattered. The word *diaspora* that some of you found in your translation means "scattered." It actually comes from a Greek verb that means "to sow" or "to scatter." Other translations use the word *dispersion*, meaning to disperse. All 3 terms work: scattered, Disapora, Dispersion. The gist of it is this: the Jews were no longer where they began. They had been scattered around the world to different places. We are certain they were feeling **just** a little bit homesick.

TOUR STOP #1 ▶ ▶▶▶

Yesterday, we left you with the Israelites in the Promised Land. If you would like to re-read those verses, turn to Joshua 13:1 and 7.

So before we connect these dots for you, we have to take a little detour to help you get the Israelites from the Promised Land to the Dispersion.

If you were reading in our Bibles, that detour would be 837 pages of the Old Testament! 😬 So we'd like you to spend the rest of the day reading from Joshua to Malachi! **#havefun #seeyatomorrow**

We are SOOOO **just** kidding! But, please bear in mind that our detour summary is covering a lotta ground!

HOLD ON TO YOUR BRITCHES

DAY 3 >> SINFULLY SCATTERED

The Israelites spent hundreds of years in an endless cycle of wandering, sinning, questioning, and repenting. They often believed they knew better than God yet quickly found out that His way would've been better. God sometimes gave them what they asked for to show them the error in their thinking. Example: they wanted an earthly king like the other pagan nations, and when they got that king, he turned out to be a living terror, causing all kinds of issues for them. By the way, this king issue was also an endless cycle: lots of evil kings, few godly ones. They turned to idol gods, walked away from their faith - sin was rampant in their lives. Many prophets like Isaiah and Jeremiah warned them to turn back to God, but their message was to no avail. The Israelites Kept. On. Sinning.

Let's pause realllll quick…before we judge them too harshly…We don't know about you, but the Israelites' journey sounds an awful lot like our lives. While our gods may not be statues, we place many things where God should be: social media, people's opinions, work, exercising, etc. We, too, have wandered from Him while begging Him to give us what we think is best for us. We, too, have discovered that His way would've been better had we **just** listened.

Okay…back to their story…

TOUR STOP #2 >>>

As a result of this cycle, the Israelites were dispersed in three different sections: Babylon, Assyria, and Egypt. Sadly, their cycle continued even during these captivities as we are going to see. We are only going to focus on the first captivity, but you can know that the other two were much the same.

Let's turn to Jeremiah 29 and read verses 4-23.

IN YOUR OWN WORDS, PARAPHRASE WHAT YOU JUST READ ABOUT THE BABYLONIAN CAPTIVITY.

DAY 3 >> SINFULLY SCATTERED

Do you recall from earlier today that the word *diaspora* comes from a Greek verb that means not only "to scatter" but also "to sow"? While the Israelites were definitely scattered, in God's sovereignty, they were also being sown exactly where He wanted them to be for that season. That is precisely what we see in verses 4-7 of Jeremiah 29. God was telling them to settle down where they were and live. They were to live in the midst of that captivity, that trial, in a way that pointed to Him. They were to care about those around them because their welfare, and the city's welfare, would be their welfare (verse 7). **Just** because they were in captivity and scattered all over did not mean His promise to them - and to Abraham, Isaac, and Jacob - was void. It was not. He was still the Faithful God they had known before.

Anybody hearing a connection to James yet?

FINAL STOP >

We don't know about you, but covering 837 pages has made our brains tired! You, too?

But before we close today, let's make one more stop. Let's connect this information to James, so we don't forget where we've been or where we're headed.

The Jews to whom James was writing are the very same Jews - generations later - that we **just** studied the past two days. One difference in the Jews then and most of us today is that they were VERY tied to their history. They knew their history well and knew how much that history affected their present. James knew this. He was a church leader, who knew that they knew about the captivities and were still feeling the repercussions of those captivities. Some of the very language he uses alludes to that. That's why he threw out the word *diaspora* from the get-go in verse 1. He wanted them to remember that he knew them, his audience, well.

Tomorrow, we are going to dive head first into the meat of James 1. There is quite a lot to digest in the few short verses we are going to tackle, but we want you to remember this history because it will help you to better understand the language James uses and where he is coming from as he writes this letter not only to these Jews, but also the Gentile (non-Jews) believers. What that means is that he was truly writing to all believers everywhere.

Just as the Jews were scattered all over (for very different reasons, mind you), we, too, as Teachers in the Word, are scattered all over. James's message is as much for us today as it was for those Jews way back then. As we begin to digest his message bite by bite, let us not forget that he is speaking to us, too. His message is applicable today no matter where we are, no matter how far we are scattered from others who are like-minded in faith. We have been sown **just** where God wants us to be, and we, too, are called to live in such a way that points to Him...**just** as James was calling these Jews to do the same.

On the next page, ask the Lord to sow the words of James into your heart as we begin to study this letter.

FAITHFUL GOD,

DAY 4 ▷▷ COUNT IT ALL JOY

So do y'all realize that we **just** took 3 days to cover verse 1 of James 1? 😅 Well, buckle up! We are going at warp speed again today! We are going to cover another whole verse!!

Before you get swept up in our whirlwind, go ahead and read James 1:1-4 in your Bible or below.

> ²Count it all joy, my brothers, when you meet trials of various kinds, ³for you know that the testing of your faith produces steadfastness. ⁴And let steadfastness have its full effect, that you may be perfect and complete, lacking in nothing.

▷▷COUNT IT

We've already talked a little bit about James's language. He is specific. He uses his literary toolbox well. #englishnerdobservation. 😎 He is doing **just** that here. As you read through the book of James, you will notice many imperatives throughout. He isn't one to beat around the bush. He's blunt. Count it. Do it. It's a command.

▷▷ALL

James reminds the Jews here - and us, too - that ALL, A-L-L, trials are giving us an opportunity to count them as joy. Not some, not most, ALL!

▷▷JOY

Once again, James's specific use of language is coming into play. If you hop back up to verse 1, you will see the word "Greetings." James is the only writer in the New Testament to use this introductory word. Wanna know what Greek word that comes from? *Chairein.* While that may be Greek to you (Nerdy *Julius Caesar* reference 😀), it is tied to the Greek word, *charis,* which means JOY. Bethany's English loving heart **just** loves James oh so much! He is so purposeful in his use of language.

The message in this one tiny word is perhaps one of the hardest pills to swallow. You see, the objects of our joy, according to James, are trials. We are to look at trials and count them as joys. There's one joy, two joys, three joys in my life right now. How hard is that??!

What shapes our view of trials is our goal. Is our goal more of Jesus? Is our goal to allow Him to prepare us for eternity with Him? Or...is our goal to live our best life now? our easiest life now? our smooth-sailin' life now? If we aim for the latter, trials will never be joyful; they'll be crushing, devastating. They will destroy us.

²Count it all joy, my brothers, when you meet trials of various kinds, ³for you know that the testing of your faith produces steadfastness. ⁴And let steadfastness have its full effect, that you may be perfect and complete, lacking in nothing.

▶▶MY BROTHERS

As we read through James, you're going to notice the repetition of this term...and it's a general one. It encompasses men and women. It's like James wants to keep reminding them that they are family.

Have you ever noticed that when you're in the middle of a trying time in life, the people you tend to treat the worst are often family members? Yep, us, too. It's easy to turn on those closest to you...mainly because we know they'll stick with us, no matter how poorly we treat them. Sad, but true. James is reminding them that family shouldn't be treated like that - stressed or not. Family needs each other. Family should support one another.

▶▶WHEN YOU MEET

The word "meet" here almost makes it sound like you're **just** takin' a walk down the road and BAM! Ya meet trials. I suppose if we're honest, that's how it goes. Trials seem to come out of nowhere. Life can be going along **just** fine when all of a sudden, a trial hits us square in the face.

The Greek definition for this word perhaps clarifies our true feelings when we meet trials. It means "to be encompassed by." It's as though we look around us, and on every side, we see trials, or the repercussions of the trial we are facing. But remember what James is commanding them: count them as joy when you meet them along life's path.

▶▶TRIALS

So what are we meeting again? We are meeting trials. What exactly are trials?

Trials are testings or proofs. They prove whether our faith is genuine or not. Trials are not temptations, exactly. As one commentator put it: "Trials rightly faced are harmless, but wrongly met become temptations." Trials can stir up in us **#somanyemotions** We often have a tendency to react to them rather than to respond. When we react, we will find ourselves tempted to sinful behaviors like unrighteous anger, bitterness, lying, selfishness, doubt, etc.

> ²Count it all joy, my brothers, when you meet trials of various kinds, ³for you know that the testing of your faith produces steadfastness. ⁴And let steadfastness have its full effect, that you may be perfect and complete, lacking in nothing.

When we respond to trials, on the other hand, we are allowing the Holy Spirit to mold us to be more like Jesus, who also suffered through many trials of His own while on earth.

When we respond, we are keeping our goal in mind - our goal to allow the Lord to prepare us for an eternity with Him. The fancy term in theology is sanctification. Our lives on earth are meant to mold us into the image of Christ.

While we're teaching you fancy theology terms, much of James' writing is considered eschatological. Eschatological refers to anything that is kingdom and heavenly-minded. In other words, James continually reminds the believers that what happens on earth has its ultimate connection in heaven. What happens on earth has a heavenly purpose.

▷▷OF VARIOUS KINDS

Trials come in all shapes and sizes. Trials may be as minor as breaking your coffee cup on a Monday morning. Although that ain't too minor...**#coffeeislife** Trials may be as major as a terminal illness diagnosis for yourself or a loved one.

All trials, no matter their size, are to be counted as joy and have the eschatological purpose of shaping up to be like the One with whom we will one day spend eternity.

We are sure that various kinds of trial - all of varying degrees - pop into your head right now. Thinking about school life, what various trials can you fit into each of the categories below?

BABY TRIALS	MAMA TRIALS	BIG DADDY TRIALS

DAY 4 >> COUNT IT ALL JOY

²Count it all joy, my brothers, when you meet trials of various kinds, ³for you know that the testing of your faith produces steadfastness. ⁴And let steadfastness have its full effect, that you may be perfect and complete, lacking in nothing.

So how do we count trials as joy? Doesn't sound so easy, does it? In fact, it almost sounds insensitive or flippant for someone to tell us to count a trial as joy in the midst of such pain and heartache and suffering. But...there's a distinction that must be made in order for us to understand James' message here: joy is not a feeling as much as it is a way of thinking. It is a faith-filled way of thinking that has our ultimate goal in mind. While joy may not be felt immediately, we can remember the promise that Psalm 30:5b holds.

Why don't you look up that verse and write it below. (Hint: The b after a number simply refers to the second half of the verse.)

That joyful morning may not come until our feet cross from earthly ground to heavenly ground, but our faith would remind us that God's ways are perfect even when we do not understand them. That is why James says that we are to count trials as joy.

Our culture today is all about **#livingmybestlife #immediategratification #easywayout #climbingtothetop #painfreeliving #creaturecomforts #comfortzone #donttellmethebad** This way of living basically ignores the fact that trials WILL come. Trials - the bad stuff - is part of living in a sinful world. And if that's the way we choose to embrace our lives, our faith will be weak, shallow, and nearly non-existent.

The problem with this narcissistic way of thinking and living is that when trials come, we don't know how to handle them because we never prepared for them. We are thrown off in a way that forever disrupts our lives and our perspective. Our lives are broken, never again to be fixed...or so it feels.

James is trying to help prepare them - and us - with his imperative in this verse: "Count it all joy, WHEN you face trials..." He did not say IF you face, so we do ourselves and our faith a disservice by living in denial of trials. However, what he will go on to say is that trials have a heavenly purpose and are meant to push us closer to our Savior and mold us to be more like Him.

If you are in the middle of a trial right now, we encourage you to listen to the song on the next page while you cry out to the Lord in prayer. If you are not in the middle of a trial right now, spend some time asking Him to prepare you for the next trial that comes or to help you properly process one from your past.

DAY 4 >> COUNT IT ALL JOY

RAISE A HALLELUJAH
BETHEL MUSIC
http://bit.ly/JustJamesRaiseaHallelujah

MY EVER-PRESENT HELP,

Let's start today by re-reading James 1:1-4. You can either open your Bible and read it or read it below.

Below, circle, highlight, star, underline - mark in a creative way, the 8 words that we focused on yesterday.

> ²Count it all joy, my brothers, when you meet trials of various kinds, ³for you know that the testing of your faith produces steadfastness. ⁴And let steadfastness have its full effect, that you may be perfect and complete, lacking in nothing.

After yesterday, are you a tad concerned that you have arrived at the end of Week 1 and we've only covered 2 verses? 😬😝 No worries! We promise not to become the long-winded professor that you dreaded in college.

Before we get too far today, we'd like you to write our ultimate goal for life that we discussed throughout yesterday. If you need to look back, you may.

Our ultimate goal is NOT to have our trials fixed. In fact, as far as we're concerned, most will not be. And even if one trial is "fixed," another will certainly come along that will not be. We must always keep in mind our ultimate goal as we face trials: to love God and know Him more fully.

Verses 3 & 4 of James 1 are the *because* for verse 2. It's James's way of stating the ultimate goal. It's like he's answering the little voices that keep asking, "Why? Why?"

Remember, we said yesterday that trials are proofs of how genuine our faith is. James is telling us that when our faith is tested by trials, the result is "steadfastness" or "patience" or in Greek, *hypomone*.

Oftentimes, we don't know our weaknesses until something in our life presses the "right" button.

Let's look at some examples:

- I may not know anger is an issue for me until one of my students says something rude, and I want to snap back rather than respond in love.
- I may not know patience is an issue for me until I explode on the student who **just** isn't getting the material that I've explained every way I know how.

- I may not know grace is an issue for me until I encounter a co-worker that doesn't do things the way I think they should be done.
- I may not know unbelief is an issue for me until I lose my job at a school that I thought was perfect for me.
- I may not know trust is an issue for me until I lose a student or watch a student suffer.

As we walk through various trials and are tested by them, not only is our faith proven genuine or immature, our weaknesses are proven to us. It's like the trials highlight the areas where we need to be molded to be more like Jesus. Until we allow Him to mold us to mirror Him in those areas, we will continue to see trials of the same kind pop up that highlight those same weaknesses. It's His way of refining us and bringing those impurities to the top so that He can rid us of them.

Our trials are also an opportunity for those around us to see Jesus work in us and through us in a way they otherwise would not witness His hand. Trials, for whatever reason, become an "all eyes on us" situation many times. Not meaning we want all eyes on us, but people tend to be drawn to watch how we handle the trial or offer their help, which gives us the opportunity to show them a little more about our Savior and how He does indeed walk through the valleys with us.

Think of someone you have watched go through a trial. How did you see Jesus working in and/or through that person?

These two verses, verses 3 & 4, remind us of the ultimate goal. Even if we can't see a trial's purpose, we can know that the trial has purpose: it produces patience in us, steadfastness, and ultimately, makes us "perfect and complete, lacking in nothing."

Those two words might have caught you off-guard: perfect? complete? I can be perfect and complete on earth? Welllllll, not quite by our English definitions. The Greek word for "perfect" is another word James likes a lot and will mention again, so it would do us well to learn its meaning.

To help us out here, let's talk all things slime. Are your kids obsessed with slime right now, or is that **just** ours? ☺ Seriously, the obsession is realllllll! If you've never made slime, we think you should check out a quick video. **Just** Google it...you'll find plenty!

When you make slime, you combine all the ingredients except the saline solution. The saline comes last, but it brings everything together into the stretchy, magical stuff these kids' dreams are made of.

While this may be a weird analogy, we think it perfectly paints the picture of this word "perfect." The slime isn't complete until you add the saline. Before the saline, the slime is sticky and terribly

Hi! I am James!

unmanageable. Even right after adding the saline solution, the slime still needs some kneading. The more it's worked and pressed and kneaded, the more manageable it becomes.

Our lives are much the same. Without trials, they're lacking something. They're lacking the very thing, the very "solution," that will bring it all together and make us what we were meant to be: mirrors of our Savior, Jesus. Trials are our "saline solution." And while trials may, at times, feel like they're making our lives more "sticky," ultimately, they're bringing all the ingredients together. The more those trials are worked and pressed and kneaded in our hearts and minds, the more we will find reason to do as James commanded and "count it all joy" as we remember God's ultimate purpose.

As Matthew Henry, a commentator, has said, "[trials] become marks of our adoption" if - big if - we allow God to mold us through them.

I don't think any of us want to be sticky and messy; rather, we want to be moldable and manageable. We want desperately to be "perfect and complete, lacking in nothing." And friends, that comes through trials. May it be our desire to...

2Count it all joy, my [Teachers in the Word family], when [we] meet trials of various kinds, 3for [we] know that the testing of [our] faith produces steadfastness. 4And [when we] let steadfastness have its full effect, [we will] be perfect and complete, lacking in nothing.

WEEK 2 ▶▶ VIDEO NOTES

Weekly videos can be found at http://bit.ly/JustJamesVideos

SCRIPTURE MEMORY: If any of you lacks wisdom, let him ask God, who gives generously to all without reproach, and it will be given him. But let him ask in faith, with no doubting, for the one who doubts is like a wave of the sea that is driven and tossed by the wind. James 1:5-6

Just as James has told us and as he will continue to tell us, prayer is vital. We all know this, but putting prayer into action daily is more difficult than we dare admit. It is easy to pray over meals and maybe pray before bed, but praying constantly throughout the day is tough. We get so focused on earthly things that bringing the heavenly things into view through prayer is quickly and sadly, all too easily eclipsed from our day-to-day thoughts. Sooo...to fix this issue, we happened upon an app that helps us to focus our minds on prayer. **#notanad #wejustloveit**

FROM BONNIE AND BETHANY

A while back, maybe two years ago, our pastor mentioned an app that he uses to help him with prayer. It's called the Echo prayer app. It's super simple to set up. What it does is alerts you - you pick the times - when it's time to pray. You can record requests and answers to prayer within the app. You can also vary your reminders based on the day, so every day can look different. It also has built-in timers that you can use to force yourself to stop and pray for a selected amount of time for whatever request popped up on your screen.

We both have it set to remind us to pray not only for friends and family, but also for our students. Bonnie has it set to remind her to pray for individual students at different times of the day since she's in the elementary world with only one set of students whereas Bethany has hers set to remind her to pray for individual classes since she's in the upper school world.

Both of us choose specific times throughout the day when we know we will have a bit of brain space to be able to stop and pray. For Bonnie, that means when she first gets to school, snack time, recess time, specials time, etc. For Bethany, that means when she arrives at school, during the students' break and lunch times, during her planning period, etc. Neither of us stop and bow our heads during these times necessarily, but we mentally stop and pray for various needs of those particular students when the reminder goes off.

It is impossible for us to be the godly teachers we desire to be apart from prayer. So setting timers to pray for ourselves wouldn't be a bad idea either. James tells us in chapter 1 that anyone lacking wisdom simply has to ask God for it, and He will give it generously. What if we all decided to set timers that said, "Pray for wisdom"? Or what if we had a timer that said, "Ask God to remind you that He hand-selected this group of students for you"? How different would our attitude and perspective be...especially if we set those timers during times of our day that we knew would be tough?

We would encourage you to join us on the **#prayertrain**. See if it doesn't make a difference for you as it has done for us.

So last week, we ended by looking at the word "complete." Slime, anyone? We know you all went out and bought **#allthethings** to make slime, right?? 😆

We did learn from slime, though. We learned that trials were the saline solution in our lives. We need trials because they complete us by molding us and making us mirror our Savior. However, we are far from complete this side of eternity...and that fact leads us right into our passage today.

Go ahead and read James 1:1-8. While you're reading, see if you can discover what is missing from our lives.

Many times, we find ourselves facing trials that we, for the life of us, cannot "count as joy" as we saw that we are commanded to do last week. Verses 5-8 offer us the answer to the *how?* How can I count these trials as joy?

What most of our English translations omit is a very important word. It's small but boasts great importance. It sits between verse 4 and verse 5. The word: BUT. Verses 4 and 5 are much more closely tied together than it may seem at first glance. You see, what we lack is wisdom...wisdom to know how trials can be counted as joy...wisdom to know how to rightly face trials...wisdom to trust God that trials have purpose. Let's see if James can help us unpack some of that *how* today.

Remember how we said James likes to use imperatives? Well, we don't get too far into verse 5 before we find one of those commands. What command do you see in verse 5?

Contrary to what we might think or what we might have been told, wisdom is not natural. We don't **just** wake up one sunny day and POOF! have wisdom. No, we must ask for it. Ya know what else is helping us to breathe a sigh of relief from this verse? What this verse does NOT say...it does NOT say that we have to be people of high-and-mighty status to ask God for wisdom. We can be **#justus** and receive wisdom from the Lord.

If you haven't raised a hallelujah yet, we think you will on this next one. Tell us how God gives that wisdom that we so desperately ask Him for...

Aside from salvation, this is one of the most precious offers God gives to us. We get generous bucketfuls of His wisdom simply for the asking! Now, yes, there is one stipulation that we're about to see, but guys...our God willingly gives us wisdom when we feel that lack and ask Him to fill in that wisdom gap. In the midst of some of the most trying circumstances, He is more than willing to give us **just** an ounce of His infinitesimal wisdom to help us understand His perspective, His purpose, His plan for our trials.

There's one more phrase in verse 5 that offers us the assurance of freedom from self-condemnation and feelings of unworthiness. James tells us that "God...gives [wisdom] generously to all <u>without reproach</u>..." Go ahead and look up the definition of "reproach." Write the definition below.

So based on that definition, what does it mean that "God...gives [wisdom] generously to all <u>without reproach</u>..."?

Soooo remember that one stipulation? We have arrived. It is in verse 6. F-A-I-T-H. We must ask for wisdom in faith. We're going to see some imagery that describes what doubt looks like, but let's hold off for a second and ask, "Faith about what?"

When looking at Scripture, it is **just** as important to note what Scripture does NOT say as well as what it DOES say. What it does NOT say here is that we are doubting God's existence, for if we are asking for His wisdom, we don't doubt that He exists. What we are most likely doubting is His character. **#ouch**

One of our favorite commentators, Kurt A. Richardson, says this: "True faith is what it is because God is who He is." What He's saying is that true faith is faith in God's character. When we doubt that He will give us wisdom to understand His perspective and His purpose in our pain, we are doubting that He is the Faithful God He promised that He is. We are doubting that He is good like He said He is. We are doubting that He is All-Knowing like He said He is. So we must "...ask in faith, with no doubting..."

STUDYING THE BIBLE TIP

When you come across a word that you do not fully understand, stop a minute, and look it up in the English dictionary.

Then, after discovering the full definition, applying the definition to the passage you're studying, ask yourself, "What is God trying to teach me about Himself in this passage?"

DAY 1 ▶▶ DON'T BE A WAVE

Imagery time!!! Guess who's excited about this dive into the literary world?!?! 😎 **#theenglishnerd**

Look back at verse 6. Below, write the 2 phrases that paint a picture of the doubter.

Not sure about you, but we don't think that imagery is very appealing. **#seasick #dontbeawave**

According to scholars, Paul viewed James as a solid church leader. James would've known about Paul's writings, and we see that Paul used a similar analogy to this one in Ephesians 4:14.

Paul and James both would've been familiar with the prophet Isaiah, who also used similar imagery in Isaiah 57:20.

Choose one of those verses and write it on the stormy, wave-rocked sea below.

What does James say the doubter will receive from the Lord?

Let's pause to remind ourselves to whom James is writing. The Jews, right? The Jews who had a history of doubting God. The Jews who doubted God and ended up wandering in the wilderness for 40 years. Yep, those Jews.

Doubting God's character is a huge deal. No wonder His Word tells us that we will receive naughta, nope, nothing of His wisdom when we doubt...because what we are doubting is Who He is.

Did you catch that imagery picture? When we doubt, it's like we are tossed from one side of supposed faith to the other side of dreadful doubt. We can't make up our minds. We aren't fully loyal to either side. We're playing the field, so to speak. That, my friends, is dangerous. And that is precisely what verse 8 is all about.

Go ahead and re-read that verse.

The name doubters are given now? Double-minded. In the original language, it is literally "double-souls." What a recipe for disaster! Matthew 6:24 is pretty clear on this as well: "No one can serve two masters, for either he will hate the one and love the other, or he will be devoted to the one and despise the other." While this verse is specifically talking about a love for money, the root is still the same: a divided soul.

We don't know about you, but the last thing we want is to lack wisdom only to be denied because we doubted God's character...we doubted He was Faithful...we doubted He was Good...we doubted He was All-Knowing...we doubted He was Loving.

Trials are hard. There's no doubt about that. God isn't asking us to pretend they aren't hard. What He's asking us to do is trust Him. And He's promising that simply for the asking, He will give us wisdom generously, without reproach. Wisdom "...not to pray so much for the removal of an affliction as for wisdom to make a right use for it." Wisdom to trust that this trial is somehow making us "perfect and complete, lacking in nothing." Wisdom to trust His character once more, knowing that He is Who He says He is.

Below, jot down some areas where you need wisdom right now.

DAY 1 ▷▷ DON'T BE A WAVE

Take the areas you listed on the previous page and turn them into a prayer, asking God to give you His wisdom regarding the trials that you are currently facing. Do so in faith.

ALL KNOWING FATHER,

STUDYING THE BIBLE TIP

Are you wondering why we keep having you read from verse one again every time we've asked you to read so far?

Well, a good study habit is to read and re-read verses in their context. Particularly with epistles (letters), the context is important as each each verse often depends upon the previous one.

...on that note, go ahead and read James 1:1-11.

Is it **just** us, or does it seem like James **just** switched gears in his letter to the Jews? It's like trials then BAM! the rich and poor. What happened there??

Well, as much as at first glance it seems that James de-railed his trial talk, verses 9-11 very much connect to verses 1-8.

Before we connect and unpack the verses, we'd like you to comb through verses 9-11 and see what they say about the rich and the poor (or lowly, as some versions say). Write the distinctions below on or around our cute little guys.

THE POOR

THE RICH

DAY 2 >> MONEY MATTERS

Do you recall from yesterday what word was omitted in most of our English translations between verses 4 and 5? If you don't, peek back and write it below.

Well, if you haven't guessed yet, that word is found yet again sitting between verses 8 and 9. It's almost as though James is saying that those who fall under the "double-minded" category need to **#listenup** as he addresses one way that we often behave in a "double-minded" way.

Let's first define the word that many of you will find in your translation of this passage. James uses the word "lowly." While this word refers to lack of monetary wealth, James also uses it to reference the spiritual state of the "lowly" as well - their humillity.

James is exhorting the poor, here, because as many of us can probably relate to from one point in our lives or another, when you are poor, your dependence on God and His provision is great. On the other hand, when you are rich, your dependence on God seems a little less necessary because of all you have accumulated.

Now, let us pause to say this - because we know what y'all are thinking...and you are correct - there are exceptions to both sides. There are poor who don't see a need for full reliance on God, and there are rich who very much fully rely on God. James is talking about the average, the norm, here.

Do you remember learning the word *eschatological*? If you need a refresher, go back to Week 1, Day 4. Write the definition below.

James is reinforcing his eschatological theme in these verses. He is reminding us that when we are heavenly-minded, thinking of God's kingdom even while on earth, we will remember that earthly things will one day fade away. What matters - and what lasts - is what we do to further His kingdom. That is precisely why he is exhorting the lowly to "boast in his exaltation," which is dependence on God, and he is exhorting the rich to boast "in his humiliation." James is urging us to remember Who we are to bring glory and honor, no matter which category we fall into.

Let's hop over to one of Paul's letters for a second. He has echoes of the same eschatological message.

DAY 2 >> MONEY MATTERS

Turn to Romans 5:3-5. Read those verses. Below, paraphrase Paul's message.

How do you think Paul's message mirrors what we have read and studied so far in James 1:1-11?

A word that is particularly intriguing in verse 9, is the word "brother." James doesn't **just** say, "Let the lowly boast in his exultation," nope. James is purposely relation-dropping (kinda like name-dropping, ya know? 😝) He wants to remind these Jews, these believers, that they are all members of the same family. And wait for it...he's not comin' down off of this soap box yet. We're going to see it pop back up in other chapters as well.

James is basically saying this: trials put us all on the same level. It doesn't matter how poor or how rich you are. When trials hit, we're allllll gonna be face down on the ground, seeking wisdom, begging for understanding. Money can't help at that point. Not all the money in the world. It goes back to what we looked at yesterday: faith. We have to get back to our roots and remember that God is Who He says He is.

Let's end today by shifting our focus a bit. While this passage can surely be applied to our personal lives, we think it's fair to say that we know of at least one - probably many, many more - families that are represented in our classrooms where poverty is a real issue. Why don't we take a few minutes and ask God specifically to use that trial to draw those families close to Him. If they can count this time as joy, what sweet fellowship they will have learned in these times of utter dependence on Him and His provision. Those will be days they will look back on as sweet memories with the Savior if they choose to have faith, believing that "He who has promised is [indeed] faithful" (Hebrews 10:23).

Also take a few minutes to ask the Lord to show you how you can minister to those families. Let the Holy Spirit guide you in knowing how to be the hands and feet and mouthpiece of Jesus as you humbly serve those that God has sovereignly placed in your path.

FAITHFUL KING,

Yesterday's verses had us wanting to break out in song: "The wise man built his house upon the rock…" Y'all know that song, right??

Well, today's verses aren't quite gonna leave us singing. **Just** wait. You'll see what we mean. But what today's verses will do…they will leave us standing in awe of God's grace and mercy and forgiveness.

Go ahead and open your Bibles to James 1. Is your Bible **just** falling open there yet? 😜

Read James 1:1-15.

You may have noticed while reading that verses 12-15 don't quite seem to be about the same subject matter. While they all fit into James's theme, we're going to go ahead and deal with verse 12 separately.

JAMES 1:12

James has clearly hopped back on the trial train here. And rightfully so…we need to understand God's purpose for trials **just** as James knew that the Jews needed to understand what they were going through as well.

James exhorts us to stand firm under trials by discussing them with that eschatological view yet again. He reminds us that when we have "stood the test [we] will receive the crown of life." That word "stood" may be a bit deceiving. The word used in the Greek will give us a better picture of what James meant. The word is *dokimos*. It is actually taken from their money making system in the ancient world. Coins were made from various metals that were heated until they reached liquid state. That liquid was then poured into molds and cooled. When cool, they would smooth any uneven edges. Some not-so-integrity-filled money changers would shave off extra and keep the excess metal to produce counterfeit money for themselves. The integrity-filled money changers learned to recognize this counterfeit money and would not accept it. These men were known as *dokimos*. They stood the test **just** as the money they accepted stood their test.

When we are in the midst of a trial, the genuineness of our faith is being tested. We can either find ourselves proven genuine or not, depending on how we stand the trial. James says that the reward for being found genuine after standing the test is the "crown of life."

Have you ever seen one of those laurel wreaths that used to be awarded to the winner of the ancient Greek athletic competitions? This would have been the "crown" the Jews most likely would've pictured, not a crown as we envision that kings wear. This crown will be awarded to those who are "approved" when trails come and is a picture of the eternal life that we will one day fully experience in heaven with Christ.

James goes on to say that those who will receive this crown are those who "love Him." "Love produces patient endurance," one commentator says, "none attest their love more than they

37

who suffer for Him." We will go to great lengths and endure much suffering for ones we love - truly love.

JAMES 1:13-15

James switches gears in these verses. His writing style is showing: blunt. He uses his words to kinda punch us. But then again, sometimes we need the gut punch. 😳

When we face trials, which James has spent the better part of chapter 1 discussing, we have a tendency to want to blame or question God. For example...

- when we experience what we deem to be unjust treatment, perhaps from a principal or a co-worker, we may want to question God's sovereignty, wondering why He would allow us to be treated in such a manner.
- when we don't get a job that we desperately wanted and thought was perfect for us, we may want to question God's provision, wondering why He would not allow us to have what seems like the "perfect" job for us.
- when we experience health struggles in the midst of an incredibly busy and stressful season in our classrooms, we may want to question God's timing, wondering why THIS time.
- when we _____,
  we may want to question God's _____, wondering why He
  _____.

It is imperative that we get James's point here. Go back and re-read verse 13.

James **just** finished discussing wisdom and the fact that we lack wisdom (verses 5-8). When we are tempted to blame or question God due to a trial, often, it is because we lack the knowledge, experience, and perspective - the wisdom - to see what God is doing in and through that trial.

Questions in and of themselves are not the issue. It's where the questions lead us that get us into trouble. For example...

- when I question God's sovereignty, I may be tempted to become bitter about being mistreated. **#sinfulanger**
- when I question God's provision, I may be tempted to turn to other things or people in an attempt to fill the void that is left, leading me right into the trap of sin. **#idols**
- when I question God's timing, I may be tempted to take things into my own hands in an effort to "fix them," which may also bring me to lie in order to cover my tracks, so to speak. **#pride**

So the question that James is answering before the Jews have a chance to ask it is - if God allows these trials into our lives, is He using them to tempt us? James gives a very definitive answer: N-O!

He quickly responds: "God cannot be tempted with evil, and he himself tempts no one."

So if God isn't tempting us, that begs the question: from where do our temptations stem?

Well...the answer ain't so pretty!

We have this tendency to want to blame Satan for everything...kinda like our students. When we ask Josiah why he cut a hole in his shirt, it is natural for him to say, "Because Ezekiel told me to do it!" They play the **#blamegame** Their parents do it, too. When we discuss a behavior issue with a parent, they want to know what every other child around their child was doing that caused their child to do something wrong. They play the **#blamegame**

You know where that **#blamegame** started? The Garden of Eden. It's not a new game. It's not a good game. It has rather disastrous results. No winners. Only losers.

Remember how we said that what is NOT in a passage is **just** as important as what IS? Well, here is another one of those scenarios. Notice that NOWHERE in verses 13-15 does James bring up Satan. Know why? Because Satan can tempt us all day long. His temptations are not the issue. The issue is our sinful selves. **#ouch** Paul said it this way in Romans 7:18: "For I know that nothing good lives in me, that is, in my flesh." We, too, have NOTHING good in our flesh. We are dirty, rotten sinners.

Soooo...our problem is our sinful selves. James reminds us that we are "lured and enticed by [our] own desire," and our desires are sinful. This metaphor is a fishing metaphor. We are baited by worm of temptation and often bite the hook of sin. What at first seemed appealing turns out to wreak havoc on our metaphorical mouths **just** as the hook slices right through the fish's delicate skin.

DAY 3 >> SIN INFESTATION

While it is not a truth we like to face, we often do take the bait. When temptations are as alluring as they often are, we have temporary memory blocks of the consequences we know follow such choices. Instead, we recall the temporary pleasure of sins...emphasis on temporary!

James paints quite the picture of what happens once we bite down on that hook. It's kinda like... GULP...lice 😬 Yeaaaaa, you read that right. We're about to talk about lice. **#youitchingyet**

Lice hide in covered areas like behind the ears and at the nape of the neck. It's like they don't want to be discovered. But lice also grow, multiply, and jump...yep, jump! They don't usually infect and affect **just** one person's head. Nope. They jump on over and have a party next door, too. **#yougrossedoutyet** Lice nits tend to cling to hair follicles, unlike dandruff that **just** flakes off. Lice are needy. They stake out land and make you pay them in your blood. They're parasites. Lice are GROSS! Can we get an amen???? **#teacherreality**

Now, if you haven't closed your book already because you were too disgusted to continue, may we draw a comparison? Sin is like those lice. Sin tries to hide itself. It grows, multiples, and yes, jumps. Sin doesn't **just** infect and affect us, it affects those around us too. Sin clings to us; it's not easy to brush off either. Sin is a parasite that makes us pay high consequences...even to the point of death. Maybe not physical death but spiritual and emotional deaths. We should be **just** as disgusted - if not more disgusted - by sin.

While we try to play the **#blamegame** or claim that Satan is the responsible party when it comes to our sin, we are the only ones that we can point to...we are the ones to blame. Seeing our sin for what it is - disgusting and horrendous in the presence of a holy God - should make us stand in awe of God's grace, mercy, and forgiveness.

Let's not forget the context for this question about temptation. James was still talking about trials and their impact on us. We must remember that questions in and of themselves are not the sinful part when asked in the right faith-attitude. However, those questions can lead us down a dangerous road, a slippery slope, where we can easily begin to fall into the temptation to sin. **#sinfulanger #idols #pride** And while it is tempting to blame Satan when we take the bait and sin, we cannot blame him. Yes, it is true that he plays a part in the temptation, and we are going to see James mention that later on, but our finger must point at our sinful hearts as we are the only ones to blame.

LET'S REFLECT >

On the next page, you will find four words that help to define the progression of sin. Define each word and then explain how each one furthers the progression of sin. Remember, this is a display of sin's progression: one thing leads to the next. Explain how these words are connected. Use what we've discussed today to help you.

DECEPTION

DESIRE

DISOBEDIENCE

DEATH

Just when you think James has talked about trials enough, he keeps on goin' like the Energizer bunny. 😆

However, what he's going to remind us today is how necessary and good - yes, good - they are.

Why don't you take a minute to read James 1:1-18.

Look at verses 4 and 17. What word do you see repeated in both?

If you remember our slime analogy, we said that **just** as saline solution is what brings the slime together, so trials are what make our lives "perfect and complete, lacking in nothing."

James repeats that exact same word in verse 17. He says that "every good and perfect gift is from above, coming down from the Father of lights…"

STUDYING THE BIBLE TIP

When you see a word or phrase repeated in a passage of Scripture, it's a good idea to pause and see why. Repetition is meant to emphasize something about that word or phrase. Repeated words or phrases are important, so mark them and meditate on them. See why they're there.

Y'all, that is an important repetition right there. What it tells us is that if God allows a trial to come into our lives, it is good for us in some way, shape, or form. It is perfecting us, molding us into His image. It is the saline solution, and He knows **just** when and where to add that saline and knows **just** how much to add. We don't know about you, but if God says something is good for us, we want it. No matter how difficult it might be at times, we want what He says is good because we need it.

Moving a little backwards here, but go ahead and re-read verse 16.

Herein lies our problem. While we may not have a problem of unbelief as Christians, we sometimes have a problem of misbelief, as one commentator put it.

We may indeed believe in God, but **just** as some of James's audience got confused, we, too, may incorrectly believe that God can tempt us or that He somehow has a part in our temptations to sin. As we saw yesterday, that is impossible.

Let's look at another verse that reinforces this truth. Turn to 1 John 1:5b. Write it below.

DAY 4 >> ONLY GOOD

In the midst of a trial, it is easy to be squeezed so much that we are then tempted to sin - often through anger or bitterness - because we begin to question God. The problem goes back to something we have discussed recently: our perspective is so limited that the pressure of the trial sometimes blinds us from God's goodness. We forget verses like 1 John 1:5 and James 1:17. We fail to remember that God is good and only good. He cannot tempt us. Any sin that arises out of a trial from us or someone else is not from God. While the trial can be from Him and the trial is what James says He uses to perfect us, the sin did not in any way come from our perfect, holy, sinless God. We talked about that yesterday.

Think back to a trial you have experienced. It doesn't have to be your biggest or worst, any trial will do. How did you see God's goodness in that trial? Perhaps you didn't see while you were in the midst of that trial, but now, looking back, you can see that He was indeed bringing good from something that was difficult.

Verse 18 brings some great relief as it sheds light on God's grace and love. The first four words are incredibly telling of God's relationship to us. Why don't you write them below.

God chose of His own volition, His own will, to bring us forth. In other words, He chose to create us. Does that not **just** make you feel loved and wanted and desired?

And not only did He "bring us forth," but He also offered us the precious gift of salvation, which brought us life.

He did all of this by the "word of truth."

Read John 17:17.

He "brought us forth...of his own will" so that we could be "a kind of firstfruits of his creatures." Firstfruits were a common thing for the Jews, and they would have recognized that word from the laws in the Old Testament. Jesus also speaks much about firstfruits. In fact, tithing is a symbol of firstfruits - giving our first and our best to honor God.

While Jesus Himself was a firstfruit of all Christians, as Matthew Henry says, Christians are a firstfruits of all creatures.

Why does that matter...and what does that mean?

It means that we are set apart as Christians. It means that we should be living lives wholly devoted to the Lord. It means that others should be able to look at us to see what Jesus is like because He is living inside of us and daily, making us more like Him.

LET'S CONNECT ► ►►

So within the context of this passage, how does verse 18 fit, you may be asking.

Think about a mom with her tiny baby. When the baby is sick, that baby is not whole. To bring healing is to bring wholeness. In order to bring healing, medicine is necessary. That medicine may come through a nasty liquid or a painful shot. That baby is not going to understand either one: gross taste or painful feeling. However, that momma knows that what she is doing for that baby is helping. It is good. In no way does she intend that baby harm.

Verse 18 is almost like a reminder that God is our Father. And even when we are like that baby - confused, hurt, ready to spit out the nasty metaphorical trial medicine, He knows that what He is doing is ultimately good for us. He is the One who breathed life into us. He is the One who chose - of His own will - to create us. And if we could **just** remember how finite our minds are compared to God's infinite mind that is full of perfect wisdom and a vast perspective, we would realize that He really is only good. We **just** aren't seeing the full picture, **just** like that baby can't understand why momma is doing what she's doing.

Listen to the song below and as you listen, take time to jot down the attributes of God that are highlighted in the song or that come to mind as you listen to the song. Use the next page to record those attributes. When you need to remember that God is only good, revisit your page of attributes to remind yourself of the truth about Who God is.

Challenge: In addition to writing those attributes, find Scriptures that back up those attributes and write them on the page as well.

NOT FOR A MOMENT
MEREDITH ANDREWS
http://bit.ly/JustJamesNotForAMoment

45

Today's verses have already made us say **#ouch** several times. In fact, we really hate to leave you at the end of Week 2 with these verses, but we think you may need a couple of days to chew on them. So...without further ado...go ahead and read James 1:1-21.

James begins with yet another imperative, but rather than asking us to do something this time, this one is like a "remember this." But it's a tough reminder, so get ready to gulp down some truth horse pills, okay?

In verse 19, you'll find three imperatives (not including the "know this" we already mentioned). List them below.

> ▷
>
> ▷
>
> ▷

These three imperatives are packed with So. Much. Let's deal with each one individually before we bring them all together.

▷ QUICK TO HEAR

The section of verses we have **just** entered focus a lot on how we can rightly handle the Word. This first portion of the imperative is no different.

It is easy to approach God's Word in such a way that we really aren't truly ready to hear. We often can be found running to God's Word, seeking to tell God what we need or what we want to see. Ultimately, in these moments, we forget that the entire metanarrative* of Scripture is about God. And when we approach His Word, our main goal should be to see what it says about Him and what He wants us to do as a result of what we see.

One commentator rewords this imperative as "hurry up and listen." Man...what a goal! What if we approached Scripture in a way that we were ready to "hurry up and listen" to what God had to tell us first and foremost about Himself?

WE FORGET THAT THE ENTIRE METANARRATIVE OF SCRIPTURE IS ABOUT GOD.

*A metanarrative is basically lots of small stories telling a bigger story.

▷ SLOW TO SPEAK

If the last imperative was convicting, this one is even more so...at least we think it is. This imperative doesn't mean we should speak slowly; it means we should be slow to open our mouths. **#yikes** The book of Proverbs is one of the places in Scripture that deals with the tongue over and over and over. Time and time again, it tells us that our tongues can bring healing, but more often, they bring hurt and death.

When it comes to reading God's Word, like we've already said, it's easy to approach His Word in a way that we want to tell Him what we need to see Him do rather than letting Him tell us what we need to know about Him. **#ouch**

James is reminding us that when we approach God and His Word, we need to listen first and speak second. It's a practice that requires more self-control than we often feel we have. We are so quick to open our mouths, aren't we? **#speakingfromexperience #justsayin**

David's plea comes to mind. Look up Psalm 141:3 and write it below.

If anyone is going to be a good watchman for our lips, it sho' ain't us! We need the Lord to be that watchman.

What if we approached God's Word ready to hear from Him, but slow to speak - waiting patiently to hear His voice, His wisdom, His character first? How much would that shape the words that did come from our mouths afterward? Wouldn't they be more loving, more grace-filled, more wise, more tender, more...God-like?

▷ SLOW TO ANGER

Remember one of our Bible Study Tips along the way...the one that said that what the Bible does NOT say is as important as what is DOES say? This is one of those times.

The Bible does NOT say, "Do not ever get angry." What it DOES say is that we should be slow to become angry. Verse 20 helps us understand why. It is very difficult for us to use anger in a way that produces any kind of good. Our anger usually crosses the sin line because we are, well, sinful. This is why Scripture over and over tells us that we need to "leave room for God's wrath" (Romans 12:19). Our anger is often destructive while God's anger is always **just** and righteous.

But again, when we look at this imperative in the context of God's Word, what James is saying is that we should approach God's Word in a way that we don't blow up because we encounter something in its pages that strikes a chord within us. **#thispassage #quicktohear #slowtospeak #slowtoanger**

What if we came to God's Word ready to hear Him? What if we came to God's Word willing to listen before we spoke? How much of our anger would be diffused if we truly had listened to what God said about Himself first? We'd learn that He is the One to whom vengeance belongs anyway. We'd learn that He would take care of those who misused us. We'd learn that He is far more long-suffering than we are and that the grace He offered to us, we should, in turn, be pouring out to those around us - whether we believe they deserve it or not. What if we were slow to become angry?

PUT AWAY ▷ ▷▷▷

Verse 21 begins with the word "therefore." It's important for us to realize how that one little word connects the imperatives we **just** studied to the next imperative that we are about to study.

Before we get too far in digging deep into the Word, "the implanted Word," as James calls it in this verse, we must address another imperative.

James calls us to "put away all filthiness and rampant wickedness." "Put away" carries with it the idea of casting off like a garment of clothing. We can't expect to jump into God's Word and discover more about Him and what He wants for us when we are clinging to filthiness and wickedness. I John 3:6 says it a different way. Why don't you read that verse? (Hint: There are 4 books bearing the name John in the Bible. The first is the Gospel of John: Matthew, Mark, Luke, John. The other three are teeny tiny books almost at the end of the Bible, next to Revelation.)

STUDYING THE BIBLE TIP

When you find the word "therefore" in your Bible, it's there for a reason. You need to stop and see what it's there for.

What James - and John - are referring to here is not attaining a sinless life. That's not going to happen on earth. But what they are reminding us is that we can't "put on" until we "put off." In other words, repentance must have a place of high importance in our relationship with God. Again, as we look at the metanarrative of Scripture to see what it says about God, we see that from the get-go, His plan was to "of his own will...[bring] us forth" and then send His Son to die as the ultimate sacrifice for our sins so that we could, one day, spend eternity with Him.

We must tend to the "put away" part of verse 21 before we can deal with the "receive" part.

What we find next in verse 21 is another one of James's favorite grammar tools: an imperative. What is he commanding us to do now? (Hint: We **just** gave the first word of this imperative at the bottom of the last page.)

```
_____

_____
```

To understand what the "implanted word" is, let's go to a possibly unfamiliar passage in Ezekiel 36: 25-27.

> 25I will sprinkle clean water on you, and you shall be clean from all your uncleannesses, and from all your idols I will cleanse you. 26And I will give you a new heart, and a new spirit I will put within you. And I will remove the heart of stone from your flesh and give you a heart of flesh. 27And I will put my Spirit within you, and cause you to walk in my statutes and be careful to obey my rules.

1 Draw a line through the things that need to be "put off." (Hint: There are 3.)

2 Underline the things that are going to be "put on" by God. (Hint: There are 5.)

3 Bracket the things that the Spirit will help us do. (Hint: There are 2.)

Number 3 is the "implanted Word" James mentions in verse 21. The Holy Spirit living inside Christians plants the word in our hearts and minds. Jeremiah 31:33 says it this way, "'I will put My teaching within them and write it on their hearts.'"

James says we are to receive this "implanted Word" with "meekness." Meekness means we need a good dose of "no self." "No self" mentality is mighty hard when we live in a world that preaches self first.

Remember, the trio of imperatives we first studied today are connected by the "therefore" to this verse. That means that in order to receive the "implanted Word" with meekness, with "no self," we must first be quick to hear what God says to us about Himself, then slow to speak, then slow to become angry. You want to know why? Glad you asked. James will answer.

Look at the end of verse 21. What is the "implanted Word" able to do?

To repeat a word that we've used several times already, James once again has an eschatological view in mind. Salvation isn't a one time process. Salvation includes sanctification, which will take place until our toes touch Heaven's ground. James is saying that the Word is what sanctifies us. It's what shows us truth when all around us is a world of lies. It's how we learn Who God is. It's how we gain wisdom. God's Word is life to us. It is our salvation.

LET'S CONNECT ▶   ▶▶▶

Soooo back to trials…when we are facing trials, trials that we do not understand, James tells us to ask for God's wisdom. But we must ask for God's wisdom in faith, not doubting. When we struggle to remain steadfast under the trial, we must remember that trials perfect us, making us more like our Savior. We must remember that every good gift is from above, yes, even trials that we don't understand. And when we face them, we must face them with the Word open on our laps and written on our hearts. We must approach that Word in a hurry to listen as God teaches us more about Himself in the midst of our trial…because don't we learn more when things are rough than when life is smooth sailing? Aren't we more apt to listen when a storm is brewing rather than when it's sunny and calm? We must be slow to speak…slow to tell the Lord how unfair we find this trial… because in our finiteness, we forget that both His perspective and purpose are so very different from ours. We must be slow to become angry because the trial **just** doesn't seem fair…and perhaps parts of it are not. But God is still God. And God is still good. Only good. We must allow Him to use His Word to bring healing to our broken places so that we, in turn, can use our broken pieces to help point the world to the only Healer.

▶▶ He is good!

WEEK 3 ▶▶ VIDEO NOTES

Weekly videos can be found at http://bit.ly/JustJamesVideos

WEEK 3

SCRIPTURE MEMORY: But be doers of the word, and not hearers only, deceiving yourselves. For if anyone is a hearer of the word and not a doer, he is like a man who looks intently at his natural face in a mirror. James 1:22-23

As teachers, we often struggle when it comes to struggling. Because we become experts in our areas of teaching, we sometimes forget what it's like to have to persevere through tough learning times. Like some of our students, it's easy for us to want to give up when we hit something that we think we should know or think we should get easily without having to strive for understanding. These times don't **just** exist within study of academic things; they also pop up in times of Bible study as well.

FROM BONNIE AND BETHANY

Waaaaay back - okay maybe not *that* long ago 😐 - when Bonnie was in seminary and Bethany was in college theology classes, we both struggled at times with material. Both of us have perfectionistic personalities that tend to tell us we should be good at everything the first time we try. This personality type also says that we should never have to ask questions. Umm…wrong. If we're being honest, both of these lies find their root in pride. We want to know everything perfectly the first time and never want to have to ask a question because we think we know it all. **#canwesayprideful** Well, once both of us realized the truth, we allowed ourselves to struggle and to ask questions, and we began the true process of learning. As Bethany tells her perfectionistic, high achievers, mistakes are part of learning. Growth requires some pain and mental yoga, and at times, that means you are going to have to try and fall and fail several times before you get it.

Bible study is no different. If we are being honest with you - and we are…we wouldn't lie to you! - both of us had read James hundreds of times before we sat down to write this study. However, some of the truths that we unpacked this time as we wrestled with the text were brand new to us. The layers of biblical understanding never end. That's the beauty of the Bible. It's inexhaustible. There is always more to be learned, always more to uncover. In the struggle of understanding came precious nuggets of wisdom that we had not uncovered before. Now, that doesn't mean we didn't do something right before; it simply means that the Holy Spirit was ready to open our eyes to these truths this time. We have wrestled for years with passages within James - looking to glean whatever lessons the Lord had tucked away in this tiny book - but it wasn't until this time as we wrote together that He was ready to reveal Himself and His truths in a brand new way. The connections we began to see were incredible!

Why are we telling you all of this? Because we think a lot of you might be like us. We don't want you to dive into passages of Scripture thinking that you should have crystal clear understanding at first glance. That's **just** not how it goes. There are some days you may pick up your Bible hoping for clarity when what you walk away with is confusion. That's okay. This is precisely why we both sit on one passage, one book, for as long as we need when doing Bible study. Sometimes, we **just** need to chew on it and meditate on it for a while. There is no shame in that.

And…you know what? Sometimes the struggle may be God's way of getting us into the shoes of some of our students, helping us to remember what it feels like to struggle.

Okay...we do promise...we are getting out of Chapter 1 this week! 😌 By the middle of this week, we're movin' on to Chapter 2. But we hope you will agree that it's been worth it. James had a LOT to say, and we couldn't **just** skate on by some of those important concepts. We needed to "chew our cud" for a bit to really pull out every last nutrient from his words.

So to begin, as normal, go ahead and read James 1:1-25.

Day 5 of last week definitely had some **#ouch** moments because talking about our tongues always carries some **#ouchfactor** However, today, we're going to find more reason to **#feeltheburn** as James camps out on a topic that is far from **#feelgoodFriday** worthy. But, you know what, the Bible isn't about making us always feel good. Yes, it holds encouragement for us. But ultimately, its metanarrative purpose is to show us the pattern of creation, the fall, restoration, and redemption over and over again (Wilkin 50). God uses His Word to sanctify us - to make us like Him, and that doesn't happen by leaving the baby in the dirty diaper. So let's not be content to sit in our dirty diapers. 😆 Let's let the Lord have His way in our hearts today.

Many commentators acknowledge verse 22 as James's theme verse. We think it's important enough for you to write it below.

```

```

1 Circle the first word in the verse. (HINT: It's a connector we've seen several times.)

2 Box the word "be." Then, write above it, "prove yourselves." (More on that later.)

3 Underline what James says we ARE to be.

4 Draw a line through what we are NOT to be.

5 Bracket what happens when we **just** focus on what we are NOT to be. (Hint: It's at the very end of the verse.)

This verse does not sit in isolation from what we **just** learned yesterday. We **just** discussed the necessity of the imperatives: "be quick to hear, slow to speak, slow to anger." We saw how James told us that we must rid ourselves of filthiness before we can the "implanted Word, which is able to save [our] souls." James is now warning us that hearing is not enough. We must do what we hear. This is how we "prove ourselves" true hearers of the Word and true followers, disciples, of Christ.

Have you ever been in desperate need of a doctor's visit? Like "I need to go now!" kinda desperate! So what do you? You go. You talk with the doctor. You listen to the doctor. The doctor prescribes you some medicine that will make you feel better. You go to the pharmacy. You pick up your prescription. You go home, set the medicine on the counter...and never take it.

That makes total sense, right? Then, 30 minutes later, you're wondering why you still feel cruddy. I mean, you went to the doctor. You listened to him. Geez...you even bought what he told you to buy. Problem? You never DID anything with what he told you or gave you. Not gonna work.

Have you ever approached Scripture like that? Because that's what James says we are in danger of doing. We may hear it, but we also may never do it. And that is dangerous and self-defeating and well, dare we say with James, plain disobedience. **#ouch**

As teachers, we know our students struggle with hearing versus listening. They hear you, all right... like Charlie Brown heard his teacher. 😄 But are they actually listening to you? Not always. And that shows when they ask you the same question you answered .02 seconds before their question.

James is very clear that when we are only hearers rather than doers, we deceive ourselves. He talked about deception once before already in verse 16, so apparently, we humans are self-deceivers. No secret there.

In light of James 1 so far, what do you think it means to "deceive yourself"?

```



```

Good 'ol Charles Spurgeon and James have something in common: they're both rather bold and blunt. We love both, though. Spurgeon said, "To deceive is bad, to deceive yourselves is worse, to deceive yourselves about your souls is worst of all." **#ouchagain**

Turn to Matthew 7. Read verses 21-27.

Much of James refers back to the Sermon on the Mount. This portion of James is one of those many times. It's as if James is echoing Jesus in Matthew 7:21-27. Spurgeon, too, was commenting on this idea: we deceive ourselves by thinking hearing the Word is enough. And he went so far as to say we are deceiving ourselves about our souls...and where we will spend eternity. But see...it's not really Spurgeon saying that. It's not really James either. It's Jesus. And man does it hurt. But it's kinda a hurts-so-good because we need Jesus to speak truth into our lives through His Word before it's too late to change. Wouldn't you agree? We'd rather hear it now than wait until it's too late.

Paul, one of James's cohorts, also mentioned this idea in Romans 2:13: "For it is not the hearers of the law who are righteous before God, but the doers of the law who will be justified."

So if our souls are in jeopardy, why do you think we deceive ourselves?

Dare we admit that it is because...
- ...hearing is <u>easier</u> than doing?
- ...hearing is <u>more convenient</u> than doing?
- ...hearing is <u>less painful</u> than doing?

It's like we want to go to church, hear the message, feel the slight sting **just** while we're sitting there, and then go on our merry way, never to think of it again or dig deeper and allow it to change us. This, too, is what James cautions us against. Go ahead and re-read verses 23-24.

How many of us would walk into a bathroom to look at ourselves, discover a giant mascara mark below our eyes, see a massive piece of lettuce stuck between our teeth, and walk out. Fix any of that? Nah. Why bother. 😝

Yet we do this with Scripture, James says. Now, yes, the Bible is more like one of those 10X magnifying mirrors with lights! It shows every. last. flaw. We see the flaws clearly, but we often **just** leave them like the mascara, the lettuce...**just** not worth fixing? Even when it's to the detriment of our souls? **#yikes** Or we see the outer issue, the surface issue, and we don't ever fully fix the problem because we don't deal with the root. Why don't we deal with the root? Because seeing that root requires time in the Word where we study and allow God's Words to probe and expose the roots. Then, **just** seeing the root isn't enough either. We have to become "doers" and actually do something about the root.

On the mirror, write some things that reading and studying God's Word might expose.

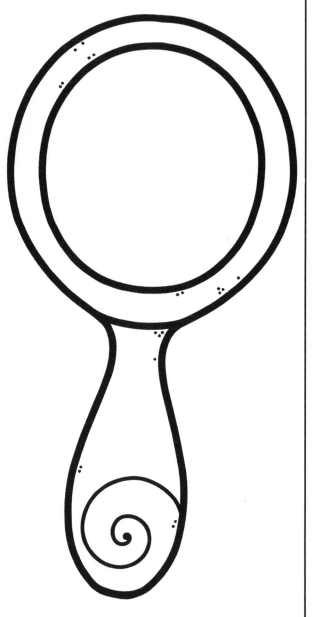

DAY 1 ▷▷ JUST DO IT

Being a true disciple means that our goal is to be like our Master. We cannot look into the mirror of God's Word, recognize something that is not like our Master, leave it, and claim that we are His disciple. It **just** doesn't work like that...says James...and says Jesus.

As the original Greek says, "...prove yourselves." Prove that you are His and that you believe His Word is truth by doing what it says. If someone told you they believed that all classroom management issues would be cured by giving every child a piece of candy to start the day, yet they never did that, you wouldn't believe them. Your answer would be: prove it (because you secretly know how absurd that idea is anyway). That's basically what James is re-iterating here. Prove that the "implanted Word" is in you by doing what it says to do. Prove to those watching you that your God is real by doing what His Word says to do.

What's interesting is that in verses 23 and 25, two different words for "look" are being used in the Greek. In verse 23, what we see translated as "looks" is a word that **just** means basically that...to look, to perceive. In verse 25, we see the word, *parakypto*, which is a much more intentional, leaned in, kind of looking. James would need two different words because the connotation is so different. The hearer simply glances in the mirror of God's Word and walks away, forgetting what he even saw because it was such a quick glance. The doer leans in and does the hard work of studying and allowing God to probe and expose. The doer doesn't easily forget what he or she saw because it wasn't **just** a cursory glance; it was an intentional examination.

LET'S CONNECT ▷ ▷▷▷

As we've already discussed, doing is not nearly as easy or comfortable or painless as **just** hearing. Doing is hard. But we must "be doers of the Word" whether we feel like it or not because the imperative gives us no caveat like "be doers of the Word only when it's convenient." It's kind of like that medicine we set on the counter. You know, the one that was supposed to help us feel better? It may be nasty. It may not be pleasant going down, but it helps to heal our bodies, so it's necessary to take, not **just** look at. Doing is sometimes like taking medicine. Sometimes doing is pleasant and we don't mind it at all. But even when it isn't as pleasant, even when it is **#ouchinducing**, it is necessary.

Remember how we learned that trials are to be counted as joy because they perfect us, making us more like our Savior? Doing has the same purpose. James says that it is "in our doing" that we find blessing. It is "in our doing" that we are being made into His likeness. He says that looking "into the perfect law of liberty" is actually freeing. Yet so often we choose to remain in our chains rather than finding freedom in God's Words.

We don't know about you, but this day has been rather convicting. We know that all too often, we are **#justhearers** rather than **#doers**, not realizing that **#justhearing** leaves us bound in chains while **#justdoing** would help us to find true freedom.

Why don't we end today by asking the Lord to probe our hearts and show us areas where we need to switch from hearing to doing.

DAY 1 ▷▷

JUST DO IT

LOVING JUDGE OF MY HEART,

Guess what? We have finally arrived at the end of chapter 1! 😎 That's the good news...

The...um...bad news? James kinda does a one-two punch in the gut deal with these last two verses. 😕 Sooo...prepare yourself.

Let's start with a question: how many of you have a hard time controlling your tongue? Raise your hand...or hands...because if you look really hard and use your **#teachersupervision**, you'll see us raising alllllll the hands over here. I mean, we will be the first to admit that our tongues get us into trouble. So, James has already stomped our toes with these verses...yes, stomped, not **just** stepped.

All right, go ahead and read James 1. Yep, the whole chapter this time. (Have you picked up on this pattern yet??? 😜)

#ouch right???

James **just** spent verses 22-25 telling us to be doers of the Word only to come back and say, "Don't get too prideful in your doing because your tongue is the true test of your heart." Yep, that's convicting.

James really discusses two different types of sin in these two verses: a sin of commission and a sin of omission.

Go ahead and define those two terms.

COMMISSION

OMISSION

Verse 26 is all about the sin of commission - we commit many sins with our tongues. Verse 27 is all about the sin of omission - we omit the imperative to take care of widows and orphans. Both sides of this coin are convicting, but if our purpose is to be like our Savior, we must stare into the mirror of His Word to understand the truth about Him first and then how we need Him to change us and shape us and mold us to be more like Him in these areas.

DAY 2 >> TRUE RELIGION

What do you think of when you hear the word "religious"?

```
[                                                        ]
[                                                        ]
[                                                        ]
[                                                        ]
```

Most of the American culture finds this word rather distasteful. Most associate it with hypocrisy, lies, or even simply **just** rote-tradition. These do NOT define what James means in this verse.

Religion, to James here, is our "doer" response to God and His Word. It should be the overflow of who we are because of Whose we are. Religion, James says, is measured by how well we restrain our tongues. Have we said **#ouch** yet???

Platt, one of our favorite commentators, says that in our techy society, this must also apply to words we type or write, not **just** ones we speak. He says, "We've created an entire culture that says if you have a thought, then you should immediately share it with the rest of the world" (28). Platt goes on to warn us that James teaches quite the opposite. How much trouble might we avoid if we were slow to begin speaking - or posting or texting or tweeting? Screens might hide us, but they don't obliterate the imperative that both James and Jesus give us. **#doubleouch**

Remember how we said that James is often quoting Jesus in his letter? Well, this is another of those times, so let's go check out a couple of verses that he is referencing.

Read Matthew 15:18 and Luke 6:45. Below, write the theme, or the main message, Jesus is teaching.

```
[                                                        ]
[                                                        ]
[                                                        ]
[                                                        ]
```

James has actually already alluded to our issue with the tongue in his own letter. Verse 19 of chapter 1 is where he told us to be "slow to speak." And now we see another layer of why...our "religion is worthless" if we do not have the self-control we need to "bridle [our] tongue."

You see, when people watch us, they are watching to see if our walk matches our talk. If we claim to be "religious" - a follower of Jesus - and yet our mouths are engaged in gossip, slander, angry talk, bitter speech, etc., we are walking self-contradictions. Now, that certainly doesn't mean that we won't ever speak or type or write an ill word...because we are sinners, but it should not be our practice, our habit, to use our tongues in that way. If it is more natural for us to speak those kinds of words - especially with no thought to how sinful it is, our heart is not right...that's what Jesus said.

DAY 2 >> TRUE RELIGION

It goes back to the Sermon on the Mount excerpt we read yesterday as well. The ones Jesus was talking about in Matthew 7:21-23 thought they were good because they were "doing" all these things, but their hearts weren't fully His. Doing things "in His name" for the sake of doing things is legalism when our hearts aren't where they should be. That's not what Jesus wants from us. He wants our hearts to be so full of Him that it is His love and grace and mercy that overflows to those around us. And that leads us right into James's next point: the sin of omission that we often gloss over.

"Pure and undefiled" religion, James tells us, is found in the hearts of those who "visit" - important word alert - the orphans and widows. Visit is not **just** a "show up and chat" word here. Visit has been translated from a powerful Greek word that implies "showing up to take care of" - the orphans and widows, in this case.

Let's look at one powerful usage of this word in Luke 1:68...**just** to solidify its power. Write that verse below.

```
```

In the context of that verse, what does "visited" mean?

```
```

Jesus didn't **just** come to "chat;" He came to rescue. James says that if our Savior's purpose was to visit the poor - aka us - and redeem them, we, too, must be about the business of selfless visiting, helping and taking care of those who are less fortunate than us.

Now, let's be clear: getting involved in people's lives can be a sticky mess. They may hurt us. They may take advantage of us. They may eventually walk away from us. However, none of that changes Jesus' command to care for them.

Notice the prepositional phrase after "to visit the orphans and widows" in verse 27. What is the object of preposition in that phrase?

IN	THEIR	

...and boyyyyy does affliction make things even stickier!

If we go way back to verse 2 in James 1, we will find the important imperative, "Count it all joy, my brothers, when you meet trials of various kinds..." Most of us have family or friends to lean on during those trial times. But orphans? Widows? Those very words scream "alone." This, my friends, should break our hearts. How in the world are they supposed to find the inner strength to face those trials with any kind of joy when they find themselves in isolation?

You see, in Bible times, a widow was to be taken in by family or otherwise was completely destitute. Ruth is an example of this type of situation.

We should be no different. As a family of believers, we should be seeking out opportunities to care for the orphans and widows around us.

Can we apply this command a little differently for our culture?
- How many of our students do we know have parents who work so much that they're basically latch-key kids who go home and spend hours alone?
- How many of our students do we know end up staying in aftercare until late, late into the evening because their parents don't get around to picking them up until then for whatever reason?
- How many of our students do we know have parents who struggle to pay the light bill or pay for a new pair of shoes for their child or struggle to pack a proper lunch for their baby because they simply don't have the money to do so?

Are they a type of "orphan"? We think Jesus would say yes.

Notice the third imperative in this verse:

1 "...bridle [your] tongue..."

2 "...visit orphans and widows..."

3 _____

It is no coincidence that these three imperatives sit together in these last 2 verses of James 1. All 3 together demonstrate true and pure religion. This last one is **just** as difficult as the first to us. Keeping ourselves "unstained from the world" is tough...especially in today's world. We are inundated with worldly ideals from TV shows and movies, social media, news, etc. We must remain vigilant about keeping ourselves aligned with Jesus by constantly staring into the mirror of His Word and checking our reflection against what we see to make sure we are reflecting Him rather than the world.

All three of these seem to connect quite easily, not only to our personal lives, but also to our teaching lives. The tongue? Yep. **#alldayeveryday** Orphans and widows? **#allaroundus** The world's muck and dirt? **#surrounded** So why don't we end today by reflecting on ways we can avoid the sin of commission and the sin of omission.

TEXT YOURSELF

1. In your **#teacherlife**, how can work on bridling your tongue?
2. In **#yourlife**, how can you visit the orphans and widows?
3. In **#yourlife**, what areas do you see the stain of the world showing up?

We may be entering a new chapter, but that doesn't mean we are leaving behind the concepts of James 1. Quite the contrary. James is going to keep expounding on different portions of chapter 1 throughout the rest of his letter.

Go ahead and read James 1:27-2:7.

Let's review the three imperatives at the end of chapter 1.

1 _____

2 _____

3 _____

The third imperative from James is the one that verses 1 through 7 of chapter 2 seems to unpack. So let's hang out there for a minute. Favoritism is a worldly trait. If true religion is "to keep oneself unstained from the world," then we must view favoritism as a sin that we flee from in all areas of life.

On the globe below, write some ways that you see favoritism showing up in our world, our classrooms, and our lives.

While James is specifically talking about the poor and the rich in these verses, his points apply to so many different types of favoritism.

For example...

 In our world, favoring our race above all others is favoritism.

 In our classrooms, favoring the struggling, high, or mid-range students over the others is favoritism.

 In our lives, favoring my preferences and my way of doing life is favoritism.

James again echoes Jesus' teachings from the Sermon on the Mount. Jesus does not condone favoritism, and neither should we.

James sets up an example of a common type of favoritism in verses 2-4. It has much to do with the rich and the poor. It is interesting to note that, immediately, the judgment begins as these two hypothetical people enter the room. Jot down some traits of each character that James has crafted for this story. (You may notice these two guys from earlier in our study, but as we said earlier today, James is expounding on chapter 1. In other words, he is adding to what he began in verses 9-11.)

THE POOR

THE RICH

According to Platt, "The word *favoritism* in the original language of the [New Testament] literally means to 'receive according to the face,' or, in other words, to make judgments based on external appearance" (33). Aren't we so guilty of that in our culture? Especially in our filter-crazed, cover-all-your-flaws, hide-behind-the-camera society? **#yikes**

What's notable here is the idea of asking the poor to sit "down at my feet." If we look at other places in Scripture, we will discover who God reserves that place for. Let's look at one example.

Turn to Luke 20:43 or Acts 2:35. Both passages are quoting David from the book of Psalms. Who will become a footstool, sitting on the ground, at the feet of Jesus?

James's audience would have been the poor who were being oppressed by the rich, which is why he spent these verses reminding them what Jesus had to say about this issue.

So not only are we - in this hypothetical example - telling the poor to sit on the dirty ground (because cement or laminate floors weren't a thing back then ☺), we are giving the poor the same seat that God has reserved for His enemies? **#ouch**

What's even more sad is that our current-day church is almost worse than the back-then version of this story James has scripted. As Kurt A. Richardson, another commentator, has pointed out, we often don't even let the true poor into our churches, much less offer them a seat - floor or pew. Richardson says, "The church's role in the world is to be redemptive, not judicial" (113). Yet we seem to be really good at judging, don't we?

What are some ways or scenarios that we are quick to have an attitude of judgment rather than redemption?

As if this hasn't been **#ouchinducing** enough so far 😐, listen to this statement from Platt: "...by neglecting the poor we are negating the grace that lies at the heart of God" (31).

Jot down your initial reaction to that statement because both of us went "unhhh" like we had been punched in the gut.

```


```

Verse 5 holds another gut punch. **Just** prepare yourselves. Side note: isn't James SO relevant for today? Goodness. We love seeing the timelessness of Scripture. 😍

According to verse 5, who has God chosen to be rich in faith? [   ] [   ]

You see, James's audience would have been the poor who were being oppressed by the rich, which is why he spends these verses reminding them what Jesus had to say about this issue. Verse 5 really should have offered them such great encouragement - you were chosen by Him to be rich in what REALLY matters, His Kingdom.

Do you hear echoes of that eschatological view again? Because you should. James is yet again emphasizing that what's important is not this world. What's important is being kingdom-minded... remembering that setting our minds on heavenly things should always be our goal. Keeping in mind the big picture, the heavenward picture, is what is vital.

Verse 6 is a quick reminder of a much more deeply-rooted issue. James says bluntly, "But you have dishonored the poor man." If we recall verse 27 of chapter 1, we will get why this sin is so egregious. True and pure religion, remember, is to care for the poor, so when we operate in a way that goes against that imperative, we don't **just** dishonor the poor, we dishonor God.

James gives his people one more reminder about the rich in verses 6-7. Go ahead and re-read those verses. We've covered a lotta ground today!

What does James remind his audience about the rich?

```


```

Is it **just** us or does the teacher in you recognize a bully situation here? The very people that we try to please and cater to - the "rich" - are the very ones who often persecute us.

Verse 7 holds an important truth for us, too. They would've zeroed in on it, too.

> ⁷Are they not the ones who blaspheme the honorable name by which you were called?

Not to oversimplify this word, because it has quite a Biblical layering of meanings, but the word "blaspheme" means "to speak evil of." Speaking evil of God's name is a HUGE deal...as we're sure you can imagine.

Think of this verse in the light of marriage: in marriage, the woman takes the name of her husband. Taking his name is a promise to him. It's a promise to love, to support, to cherish, to walk alongside until "death do us part."

In the language of the Bible, salvation is much like a marriage - only there is no "death do us part" because death will in fact bring us together with the very one we have pledged to live for. In salvation, we have taken God's name as our own, Christian. We represent Him. We have promised to love Him, to obey Him, to cherish Him, to walk alongside Him.

These rich people, according to James, are defiling the very name the Jews, as well as you and I, have taken when we received Christ. Catering to the rich and refusing the poor makes no sense in light of this fact. Why would we cater to the very ones who defame our Savior's name?

Just so that we are all on the same page, let us stop briefly to say - riches don't equate to evil. Rich people are not all evil. Nor are all poor people godly. However, as the narrative of Scripture teaches us, it is often harder to live a life "unstained by the world" when we have enough money to afford many worldly things. What the Bible tells us is that when we have been blessed in ways that cause us to be considered "rich" in earthly terms, we have a great responsibility to use those blessings in a godly way - in a way that showcases Jesus.

LET'S REFLECT ▶ ▶▶▶

Think about your classroom. Is it set up in such a way - your seating, your lessons, your schedule - that you are showing favoritism to one type of student or another rather than considering all students equally? We know that we are all most likely guilty of this in one way or another. So how can we change that? How can we make sure we are not guilty of favoring one type of student over another? What changes do you need to make in your classroom to fix any of these errors?

On the next page, jot down your thoughts and ideas.

You know what's comin', right? 😜

Go ahead and read James 2:1-11.

James is continuing his gut-punch discourse on the poor vs. rich saga. What does he seem to be reiterating again in verses 8-11?

Before we can move too far along in these verses, we must deal with this "royal law" that he is referencing. The Jews would have known exactly what he was talking about, so let's make sure we do, too.

Turn to Leviticus 19. Read verses 15-18. (For those of you new to the Bible, Leviticus is the third book in the Bible, so go waaaaaaay to the end that is opposite from James.)

Are you hearing the echoes of what James has been teaching? They are loud and clear in those verses!

The royal law is found at the end of verse 18. Why don't you write it below. (Hint: It begins after the conjunction, but.)

Let's get a little nerdy...English nerdy for a second. 🤓

There's a fun literary term - okay fun to Bethany - known as metonymy. Metonymy is where one word represents something that is related to it or comprises all the parts of it. Confused? Hang on. Example time. If I say: The table laughed at his joke. The table actually represents all of the people sitting around it. **#metonymy** Or if I say: The Bulldogs were up in the game. The Bulldogs represent all of the players on the Georgia Bulldogs team. **#Bonniesfavoriteteam #metonymy** Get it?

Why does that matter? Because that's what James is doing here. The word law is representing all the individual laws the Jews would've known. Leviticus actually holds many of those laws. Keep that in mind. It's going to be important in a minute.

If the royal law tells us to "love [our] neighbor[s] as [ourselves]," it would be important for us to know what kind of love James is talking about. *Agape* is his word of choice. Greek has a plethora of words for love, so his choice is vital. It was purposeful. He didn't opt for the friendship love word, *phileo*. He didn't opt for the romance love word, *eros*. He opted for *agape* - the self-sacrificing, my-life-for-yours kind of love word.

How does that definition - of a sacrificial kind of love - impact the meaning of loving your neighbor as yourself?

Truly loving our neighbors is hard. Especially when we consider that loving our neighbor does not mean loving neighbors who are like-minded necessarily. It doesn't mean loving only the ones who are Christians. Neighbor **just** means people. We are to love people as we love ourselves.

So what about your teaching neighbor? You know, the one next door or down the hall from you. Are you loving that neighbor as you love yourself?

Admin? Parents? Yep, even the one that emails you 473,892,407,329 times a week. Students?

How are you showing that sacrificial love to those neighbors? Or if you aren't currently, how can you begin showing them that kind of love? Take a minute to jot down ideas on the door below.

It is so easy to get wrapped up in our to-do lists, isn't it? So much so that we don't even think about loving our school neighbors in the most simple of ways: offering to make their copies, offering to cover a duty for them, offering to watch their class for a few minutes, writing them a card.

When we are required to sacrifice something of ourselves - our time, our money, our energy - we can be sure that agape is at work in us when our heart's desire is to be like our Savior through that action.

Verse 9 is where James starts that one-two punch action again. Prepare yo'self. 😬

James says that when we show partiality - the same idea that he unpacked in verses 1-7 - we commit sit and are transgressors, or lawbreakers.

That word "partiality" means to be an "outward respecter." In other words, we show favoritism based on what we see on the outside of a person.

THE TEACHER NEXT DOOR

When we treat others with partiality, it is not treating them like we would treat ourselves. Despite what we'd like to think, we would never treat ourselves in the way we often treat those we feel are lower than us. That is breaking the royal law, James says. That is sin.

And even if we don't outwardly show that partiality, Matthew Henry would remind us that our thoughts would tell on us: "The deformity of sin is never truly and fully discerned till the evil of our thoughts be disclosed."

Remember that metonymy device? Here's where it is important. Verse 10 tells us that all it takes to be consider a lawbreaker is failing - or more literally defined as "falling" or "tripping" - in one part.

Think about it: we don't have to break every one of our country's laws in order to be a lawbreaker. If we speed, we are a lawbreaker. Now, we try to level the "breaks," if you will. "Well, I was only going 5 over. That's not as bad as so and so who was caught going 30 over." Both parties are still lawbreakers. The degree does not matter.

That's precisely what James is saying. The law represents allllllll these parts. You break one, you've broken all.

For those who spend their lives trying to save themselves, this becomes quite the problem. How can you fix that issue? How can you atone for breaking every law in your short stint on earth? The answer is simple: you can't. And that is why we are in desperate need of Jesus, Who died once for all. The Cross was enough to cover every sin. His blood was the atonement for every law that He knew we would break.

Verse 11 is tough. For some of us, it's one we gloss right over, feeling no conviction because we have committed neither of those sins - or so we think - that are listed. For others, it may bring heavy conviction and waves of guilt because we have committed one of those sins.

Let's define those two words. How would you define adultery and murder?

ADULTERY	MURDER

We are going to play a guessing game and guess what many of you probably wrote.

For adultery, we would think that most of you put something along the lines of breaking the marriage covenant by being unfaithful to your spouse. Yes?

For murder, we would think that most of you put something along the lines of taking the life of another person. Accurate?

Let's peel back another layer, though. Words often have layers of definition **just** like onions. Onions have those fine, thin layers that are almost see-through they're so fine. Let's see through the surface layer to the next and peel off another layer of these definitions.

See if you can come up with a different level of meaning for each of these words.

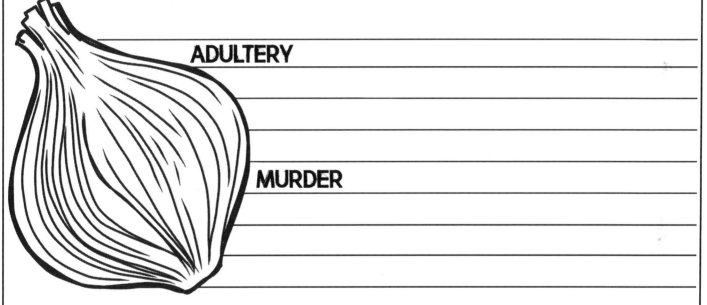

ADULTERY

MURDER

James is going to re-visit both of these terms later in his book, in chapters 4 and 5. However, it would behoove us to stop and understand the other definitions or connotations that he is using here and in the coming chapters.

Spoiler alert: chapter 5 is going to deal with how the rich have oppressed the poor. James is going to talk about the punishments that will come to them. In chapter 5 verse 6, he says something interesting. Go ahead and read it. Which of our two words do you see in that verse?

ADULTERY   MURDER

Jesus talks much of helping the poor in the Gospels (Matthew, Mark, Luke, and John). He clearly tells us that we should be giving to the poor. He often tells those who want to follow Him that they should sell everything and give their possessions to the poor. He also says that if one who is poor needs food or clothing and we **just** say, "Go in peace" without helping them, that is useless because we have the power to help them, yet we are choosing to do nothing. What James does is connects these teachings of Jesus with this word: murder.

While at first glance this connection might seem harsh, it is truth. James is saying that when we neglect the poor and do not aid them by helping to provide for their basic needs, we are, in essence, murdering them (Richardson, 123). Does that sting as much for y'all as it does for us?

But **just** on a very surface level, can we not honestly see how that connection can be made? If someone can't afford proper food and clean water, they can't go on living but so long. Without proper shelter, they will only live for a certain amount of time. When we have the ability to help the poor with such basic necessities of life, James - and Jesus - says that we <u>must</u>. It is an imperative to us: give.

As for adultery, as we will see in chapter 4, he is going to go back to that marriage metaphor that we talked about yesterday. Salvation is often compared to the covenant promise of marriage in the Bible. When we give ourselves to the world rather than giving ourselves to God, we commit spiritual adultery. More on this one in chapter 4.

While it's easy to see these words and, at first glance, think we have no connection to them, upon further peeling back those layers, it is safe to say that we have all committed both and should feel that convicting tug of the Holy Spirit on our hearts.

Let's end today by spending some time in Jesus' presence. Let's not be quick to let the Holy Spirit's conviction pass without dealing with what He's bringing to our minds and hearts right now. While you listen to this song and reflect on the words, color. Then, on the next page, write your heart's cry of repentance right to Jesus.

NOTHING ELSE
CODY CARNES
http://bit.ly/JustJamesNothingElse

CAUGHT UP IN YOUR PRESENCE

JESUS, I'M SORRY...

This week has been one of gut-punches and heavy conviction, hasn't it? Or maybe that's **just** us.

Conviction is good. It means our hearts are soft and pliable. It means we are open to what the Holy Spirit wants to show us and how He wants to change us.

We have need to be concerned when we no longer feel His conviction in our hearts.

Before we dive too far in, go ahead and read James 2:1-13.

Here we find yet another imperative. Go ahead and circle the two words that we find in this imperative statement in verse 12.

> ¹²So speak and so act as those who are to be judged under the law of liberty.
>
> ¹³For judgment is without mercy to one who has shown no mercy. Mercy
>
> triumphs over judgment.

Do you recall studying about speaking before? That should ring a bell. James 1:19 and 26 both speak about speaking and the tongue. Remember that we said that verse 19 wasn't only talking about interpersonal relationships but also was speaking about approaching Scripture. We are to be "quick to hear, slow to speak, [and] slow to [become] angry" as we read verses that may be incredibly convicting to us. Verse 26 reminded us that anyone who could not bridle his or her tongue had worthless religion. **#stillanouch**

James is unpacking those ideas a bit more in these verses. This imperative is telling us that we are to speak and act - two very clear actions - as those who have been set free and therefore should view others in light of God's mercy and grace which He showed to us.

James already made it clear earlier in chapter 2 that we have a tendency to be judges although that is not our job. Here, he reminds us that when we act without mercy as we deal with others, it won't go well for us later on.

Let's define two words. Very different words from yesterday! 😄 If you need to use a dictionary, go right ahead.

OPERATIVE	**VERBAL**

James spends the better part of his letter reminding us that there is a HUGE distinctive between an operative faith and a verbal faith. So in that context, after defining those words, what do you think the difference is between a person who has an operative faith versus someone who has a verbal faith?

In the remainder of chapter 2, we are going to see James present the argument of faith versus works. But these two verses are a glimpse into his next point.

When we claim to have Jesus living in us yet become judges of others rather than loving them and showing them the same mercy and grace that we have received, we deceive ourselves. We have only a verbal faith.

If we had an operative faith, our words and actions would overflow with mercy and grace.

Let's use a hypothetical scenario for a minute...one that might not feel so hypothetical because we all can probably fill in the blank with a real name.

Imagine that you have a student who consistently misbehaves. We're talking all day every day. Over the top. Nothing seems to stop this student.

If you were to respond with a verbal faith - one that judges rather than loves, one that is more void of mercy than it is full of mercy, what kind of response might you give to this student?

Now let's flip that. If you were to respond with an operative faith, one that loves rather than judges, one that is full of mercy more than it is void of mercy, what kind of response might you give to this student?

We aren't going to have you answer this on paper, but think for a minute on this: which response is your norm? Verbal or operative?

Verse 13 is oh-so-convicting once we know which one we are. Go back to page 75 and underline how we are judged if we do not show mercy to others.

Ouch, right?

You see, James is telling us that the natural response to God showing us so much mercy is that we should be full of mercy - merciful - to the point that mercy **just** spills out of us, overflowing to those around us.

Turn to Romans 2 and read verses 6-11.

After you've read those verses, unpack what will be given to each: the self-seeking individual "who does evil" and the kingdom-seeking individual who seeks to do good.

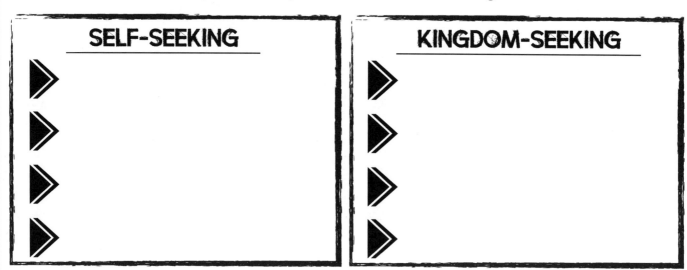

SELF-SEEKING
▷
▷
▷
▷

KINGDOM-SEEKING
▷
▷
▷
▷

The Gospel is a perfect example of the last four words of James 2:13. Go back to page 75 and box those last four words.

When Jesus died on the Cross for our sins, His mercy was triumphing over our fully deserved judgment which said that the only payment that would do to cover our sins was death. His merciful death triumphed over that judgment sentence and gave us victory.

The same is true for us as we learn to love our neighbors as ourselves - back to the royal law that encompasses all the other laws. When we look at others through the eyes of mercy, we learn to remove the harsh judgment which our world and our sin natures have taught us to use. Rather than looking on them with eyes that judge and showing partiality or favoritism, we learn to look at them with the same eyes Jesus has when He looks at us: eyes full of grace and mercy and forgiveness.

Seek Mercy

List some ways that you could be a more merciful teacher this school year.

▶

▶

▶

▶

▶

▶

WEEK 4 ▶▶ VIDEO NOTES

Weekly videos can be found at http://bit.ly/JustJamesVideos

SCRIPTURE MEMORY: So also faith by itself, if it does not have works, is dead. But someone will say, "You have faith and I have works." Show me your faith apart from your works, and I will show you my faith by my works. James 2:17-18

When Bethany teaches writing, one of the things she teaches her students is that the first time something is mentioned, it needs to be explained or written out fully (ex. an author's name, a character, an allusion to a historical event, etc.). But the next mentions don't need to be as complete because they've already been introduced. The next time, **just** the last name of the author or the character's name or the historical event can be said without repeating the background material again. The same is often true within Scripture.

FROM BONNIE AND BETHANY

There is something called The Law of First Mention. This is a Bible study term that simply means that when something is first mentioned in Scripture, it is often padded with extra information or there are important concepts included that won't necessarily be given the other times it is mentioned.

For example, in James, he mentions multiple Old Testament characters. Well, The Law of First Mention would teach us that we should go back to the first time those characters are mentioned in the Bible to see who they are and what they were all about. When we take the time to find the first time they are mentioned, we often uncover some valuable information about them.

The same is true for words. When I encounter the word *righteous*, for example, it may be helpful for me to use a simple search bar in a Bible app to see when the first mention of this word was. I may **just** find some valuable insight when I look at the context of the first use of a word.

If you are a person who journals, this would be a good practice to add to your journaling. When you come across words or people or events as you study Scripture, jot down where you found it, but then, find the first mention and paraphrase or bullet point list what you learned from that first mention.

If you're not a person who journals, we'd encourage you to try this as well. Any time we can force our brains to paraphrase information that we've read, our brains retain that information better and for longer periods of time. Even if you paraphrase on a sheet of paper that you'll toss, that's fine. The process of writing it out is what allows your brain to hold onto it.

You also may find it helpful when looking up the first mention to go back to other places that the word or character or event was mentioned **just** to see the various uses of it. These are known as cross references.

¹⁴What good is it, my brothers, if someone says he has faith but does not have works? Can that faith save him? ¹⁵If a brother or sister is poorly clothed and lacking in daily food, ¹⁶and one of you says to them, "Go in peace, be warmed and filled," without giving them the things needed for the body, what good is that? ¹⁷So also faith by itself, if it does not have works, is dead. ¹⁸But someone will say, "You have faith and I have works." Show me your faith apart from your works, and I will show you my faith by my works. ¹⁹You believe that God is one; you do well. Even the demons believe—and shudder! ²⁰Do you want to be shown, you foolish person, that faith apart from works is useless? ²¹Was not Abraham our father justified by works when he offered up his son Isaac on the altar? ²²You see that faith was active along with his works, and faith was completed by his works; ²³and the Scripture was fulfilled that says, "Abraham believed God, and it was counted to him as righteousness"— and he was called a friend of God. ²⁴You see that a person is justified by works and not by faith alone. ²⁵And in the same way was not also Rahab the prostitute justified by works when she received the messengers and sent them out by another way? ²⁶For as the body apart from the spirit is dead, so also faith apart from works is dead.

If you haven't already, grab your Bible and read James 2:1-26. Read slowly. There's a LOT packed in there. And no worries if you start to feel a little like this guy toward the end ☺...we are about to spend three days unpacking verses 14-26, so we will get well-acquainted with them! ☺

While James **just** warned us that judging others without mercy is not going to end well for us because it will cause us to be judged without mercy, he has NOT told us that we are not to judge ourselves. In this section of chapter 2, James is asking us to take a good, long, hard look into our hearts and judge our own motives and actions to determine where we really are spiritually. We're gonna be real: some spiritual surgery is about to take place. Get ready to put your life, your heart, your soul under the microscope of God's Word.

Over the next three days, we are going to ask you to return to page 81 several times to mark up this passage. You may want to paperclip it or something...make it easy on yourself! ☺ So, to begin, in verse 14, circle the two things (nouns) that James is discussing.

While James is indeed writing to a very real audience, the Jews of the Dispersion, in this chapter, he is utilizing an argumentative technique that English teachers teach students to use when writing an argumentative essay. He does it a little differently than we might expect in a paper, but he does it well, nonetheless. He acts as though he is having a conversation with someone. While conversing with this imaginary person, he anticipates all of their questions and offers refutation to the points this invisible person would most likely bring up. So as we dive into this passage, keep this hypothetical person and conversation in mind.

VERSE 14

James begins with a two-part rhetorical question. The biblical answer to this question is of utmost importance because the question hinges on salvation.

Put both parts of his questions in your own words.

According to James, it is possible to believe we have faith yet not truly have it at all. James says that the way we test to see whether or not we have faith is deeds, or works.

If you'll remember back to James 1:22-27, James really said the same thing in different words. He told us that we need to be "doers of the Word, and not hearers only, deceiving [ourselves]." He went on to say that taking care of orphans and widows was part of what defines true and pure religion. In fact, remember that he went so far as to say that when we don't, we are proving our religion worthless. **#stillanouch**

If James 1 was his thesis, we can expect him to keep re-visiting the same topics and truths from that chapter as he is right now. He is reiterating the fact that when our works - our actions - don't match our words, we have every reason to question if the faith we claim to have is real and living in us or if it is fake and dead.

Since we've gotten to know James a bit over the past few weeks, how do you think he expects this imaginary person he is speaking with to answer those rhetorical questions in verse 14?

VERSES 15-16

If we didn't know better, we'd think James had **just** jumped ship from his first topic and hopped onboard another ship. However, if we've learned anything about James, it's this: he introduces a topic only to expound on it later and then tie up all the loose ends when he's good and ready. This is one of those spots.

James seems to have jumped backwards to the 1:27-2:13 ideas about caring for the poor and not showing favoritism based on outward appearances. And in some ways, yes, he is referring back to those principles. But upon closer look, he's expounding further on verse 14.

He **just** said in a rhetorical fashion that if our faith is real, our works will back that up. Yet how often do we do the modern day Western version of what verses 15-16 are expressing? Too often.

Head back to page 81.

- Pick a color. Any color. Highlight two things the brother or sister is in need of in verse 15.
- Then, draw an arrow to what this imaginary person James is talking to says to "fix" these issues (verse 16).
- Lastly, bracket James's rhetorical question at the end of verse 16.

In the time period James lived, this "Go in peace, be warmed and filled" was a common farewell greeting. It was kind of the equivalent to our modern day, "Have a nice day!" But here, James is calling motive into question. He's saying that we need to put our hearts under the microscope. Do we really think that telling someone who cannot clothe or feed him/herself because of poverty to "Go in peace, be warmed and filled" without doing a thing to help them is okay? Again, he would anticipate a hearty, "No," to his question.

Y'all, this is convicting to us. We're sure to you, too. How often do we speak a modern day equivalent of that phrase without truly meaning a word of it? How often do our actions not match our words?

On the flip side of this hypothetical encounter with a brother or sister who is poor, James would say, what we really should do is help them. Feed them. Clothe them. Give out of our abundance.

Let's take a look at some of Jesus' words. Turn to Matthew 25. Read verses 35-40. Keep in mind as you read that the King mentioned is Jesus.

How does He say that we minister to Him? (Hint: Verse 40 holds the answer.)

James - nor Jesus - asks us to fix every problem created by poverty. But what they do tell us is that we are responsible to do what we can. Our love for Jesus, the fact that He is SO worthy of our devotion, our obedience, our love, should make us want to take the love and mercy and grace He showed to us and pour it out to those around us. For after all, as Spurgeon said, "it [is] the sweetest thing in the world to do anything for Jesus."

As teachers, we encounter a lot of families, maybe even co-workers, who struggle with poverty on some level. What are some practical ways you can take your abundance and help those facing poverty?

> The saints fed the hungry and clothed the naked because it gave them much pleasure to do so. They did it because they could not help doing it, their new nature impelled them to it. They did it because it was their delight to do good...They did good for Christ's sake, because it was the sweetest thing in the world to do anything for Jesus.
> Spurgeon,
> "The Final Separation," 288

VERSES 17-18

Go back to page 81. Put an X over the very last word of verse 17. Then, come back and spell out that word in the boxes below.

As simplistic as this sounds, when something is dead, it does not have life. Something dead doesn't have *some* life. It has NO life at all. James tells us in verse 17 that when we claim to have faith, yet we have no works - no overflow of Jesus spilling out of us - that faith we claim to have is dead: D-E-A-D. In other words, it was never real faith to begin with.

Living faith is active faith. Remember our two words from Day 5 of last week: operative and verbal? Same concept here. If we truly have faith in our Savior, we will have an operative faith. We will show that faith by how we live and act and walk.

STUDYING THE BIBLE TIP

As any student learning something new will admit, learning is HARD! We don't want you to think that studying the Bible is always going to be super easy. Studying the Bible is learning, and sometimes it is difficult. This passage, actually all of James, has some tough stuff in it. It is 110% okay if you struggle...in fact, it's 110% okay if you're wrong at first. Allow yourself to learn to "love the Lord your God with all YOUR mind." And sometimes, that's going to mean not knowing the answer or getting the answer wrong. We promise to help you unpack the truth - even if it comes a little later in the study. Just hang tight.

Verse 18 brings back the imaginary person to whom James is speaking. James imagines that their rebuttal to him would be, "Fine. You have faith. I have works. What's the big deal?" So James rebuts yet again.

Go back to page 81.

In verse 18 - focusing on James's rebuttal after the imaginary person's comment that we **just** looked at above, underline the two phrases that James uses to describe how these two imaginary people are supposed to prove their faith.

If the one who claims to have faith apart from works can't use works to prove his or her faith, what's left? How do you think they would prove their faith?

We aren't sure what you came up with, but the only thing we can come up with is words. They'd have to use words. And we're not sure how great that's going to work either. Because...let's be real...sometimes, we use a lotta words that have no meaning.

Example #1: We tell our students over and over and over that if they don't stop talking, we will write them up, clip them down, take away DOJO points...whatever the punishment, yet they keep on talking, and we **just** keep on warning them.

Example #2: We stand around the coffee pot or sit in the teacher workroom and discuss how we think active learning is best for our students, yet we don't change the way we teach one iota.

In either case, what do our words prove? Probably that we don't truly mean or believe either. If we really believed what our words were saying, our actions would back them up.

The bottom line, James says, is this: we can try all day every day to prove we have true faith APART from works, but it ain't gonna happen.

So how do we prove our faith - how do we demonstrate how real our faith is? BY our works.

James isn't saying works save us. James is saying that works prove that Jesus has taken up residence in our lives and changed our hearts. Works should be a natural outflow of the love and grace and mercy that Jesus has shown to us first.

When faith is real, actions will prove it.

Remember how we said spiritual surgery was about to take place? Well, now's the time.

> Stated Belief
> + Actual Actions
> Actual Belief
>
> Mark Liederbach

Let's end today by reflecting on areas that we are proving our faith to be real because our actions actually match what we say we believe. But let's not stop there. Let's also honestly evaluate where we're struggling.

On the next page, list some areas where your faith is actionable - it's working itself out, so to speak.

Then, list some areas where you're struggling...where perhaps the action is missing from your words.

Spend some time in prayer, asking the Lord to help you add action to those areas.

MY FAITH IN ACTION

MY FAITH NEEDS ACTION

Yesterday had some tough theological "put-on-your-big-girl-pants" kind of information! We are quite sure, like us, your brains were a bit exhausted...if not from the information, from the spiritual surgery that was started. 😣

We are going to continue to build on yesterday, but before we get too far, go ahead and re-read James 2:1-26.

Do you recall the equation we put in a quote bubble for you yesterday? If so, fill in the blanks below. If not, turn back and re-read it, and then fill in the blanks.

As we saw yesterday, our faith is dead, D-E-A-D, if our works aren't actually working, proving that what we *say* we believe is truly *what* we believe.

Today, James is going to continue in that same vein of thinking. Remember, that in this section of chapter 2, he is talking to the imaginary person who doesn't quite agree with him.

VERSES 19-20

In verse 19, James jumps a bit again. It's like we missed hearing what the imaginary person said, but we can tell a lot based on James's response. This imaginary person seems to be continuing to argue that he or she can indeed prove the realness of faith by words alone. James combats such statements by responding, "You believe that God is one; you do well!"

Is it **just** us, or can you sense the sarcasm? **#yikes**

James begins here what author, David Platt, sees as a 3-part understanding about faith:

- Faith is not mere intellectual assent.
- Faith is not simply an emotional response.
- Faith involves willful obedience.

Let's unpack each one.

Faith is not mere intellectual assent.

Go back to page 81.

Box who James says even believes in God.

Then draw an arrow to their response.

DAY 2 >>> FAITH THAT WORKS

Demons, according to James, are not confused on who God is. In fact, "[e]ven the demons believe" in Him, James says. The problem is that their belief stops there. It's purely intellectual. That's it. No works back up what they claim to believe.

Faith is not simply an emotional response.

The demons do have one response: they shudder. However, this is simply an emotional response.

Have you ever experienced tears in your classroom? Sometimes, especially early on in our teaching careers, tears are scary. We fear we have gone overboard or done something terribly wrong because "no child in my class should ever cry," we tell ourselves. However, tears are often a sign of remorse and brokenness, which is the beginning of repentance. Tears aren't always a bad thing.

Butttt, is it **just** us, or have you, too, had students use tears as a way of manipulation? You know, Tucker **just** wants you to say that he really did have that toy first, and his friend, John, shouldn't have it right now, so the tears roll, and the sob story begins as Tucker tries to work his way out of time out with those tears.

Or silent lunch or detention is given to an older student who has been disrespectful or repeatedly disobedient, and while serving that consequence, the tears roll. Upon seeking an answer for the tears, you discover the child isn't sorry about the action but rather is upset about the consequence he or she is now facing and perhaps the one that may await them at home.

Emotional responses aren't evidence of true faith. "...Even the demons believe—and shudder!"

Faith involves willful obedience.

Let's head to the Greek for this one. The Greek word for faith is *pistis*. The root word that helps to make up this word is one that means "persuasive power."

We have an English word that finds its roots in this word as well: *piston*. Any idea what a piston does? In layman's terms, it makes a machine go. Your car engine would not move without a piston; it would remain still. Pistons make engines or machines move.

James says that faith, *pistis*, should make us move, too. Faith isn't about being still and simply using our words to say we have faith. No, true faith makes us move; it sends us into action.

In verse 20, James gets a little - shall we say - bold? Check out what he calls this person. Head to page 81 and circle the name he chooses.

James upped the ante here. His word choice is a bit more specific. He is reaching the pinnacle of his argument. He now says that faith without works is what?

This isn't new news. He's said before that "faith without works is DEAD," but apparently, this imaginary person…who seems very much like some real people in our world - perhaps even us at times…this person **just** isn't getting it. So rather than repeating himself again, James switches up his words and says, "It's useless!"

But, let's pause for a second and ask ourselves: what would be the point in having faith if it didn't change something in us? What would be the point in believing something that didn't spur us to some sort of action? What good would it be to believe in God's existence, yet never alter the way we viewed the world or treated the people He places in our paths?

Faith without works is useless.

VERSES 21-24

James turns over another leaf here. He branches off into some examples of those who demonstrated their faith by their works. Abraham is the first.

If you are unfamiliar with the story of Abraham and Isaac, or if you **just** need a refresher, turn to Genesis 22:1-19 to check it out.

Lest we forget the bigger picture of James, let's head back to James 1:2-4. Re-read those verses, this time, keeping in mind the story of Abraham and Isaac.

Abraham's story is one of trial and perseverance. But before we unpack that, there's one biblical history point that would be helpful for us to understand.

The Jews were bombarded with false gods. Nothing new. We are, too. Ours **just** don't always come in the form of metal statues as theirs did. One in particular we need to meet. The name of this god was Molech.

According to Charles Patrick, an adjunct professor at Southwestern Theological Baptist Seminary, Molech was "an Ammonite god who required propitiatory child sacrifice. A couple sacrificed their firstborn by burning the child on a metal idol of Molech, believing that Molech would ensure financial prosperity for the family and future children. The Israelites were strictly forbidden to practice this form of worship (Leviticus 18:21, 20:2-5; 2 Kings 23:10; and Jeremiah 32:35)."

First of all, how disturbing is that image?? Burning your child for an idol?

But secondly, how odd of a request for God, the One True God, to make of Abraham in a culture of Molech sacrifices.

As Richardson says, "[This] is a story about what God does NOT want as much as about what He wants. Unlike the other gods of the nations, the God of Abraham wants true faith, not the death of sons" (139).

DAY 2 >> FAITH THAT WORKS

We see zero hesitation in Abraham as he is told to take his son to the mountain. We see zero hesitation in Abraham when Isaac asks where the sacrifice is. In fact, Abraham's response to his son speaks volumes about his faith: "The LORD will provide."

James 1 teaches us that perseverance in the midst of trials has purpose. Its purpose is to produce in us steadfastness, which then will leave us "perfect and complete, lacking in nothing." How do we visibly see perseverance? In our works.

"Abraham's actions were his perseverance in faith" (Richardson, 140). If Abraham's faith had not been real, he would never have packed up with his one and only son - whom he had prayed for for years, mind you - and headed up that mountain. Faith that isn't real doesn't act.

Abraham was being a "doer of the Word" to use James's words.

Head back to page 81.

Look at verse 22. Underline the two things that Abraham's "faith was..." in that verse.

Do you hear the echoes of the very same words James used in 1:2-4? If our faith is tested by trials, and if our perseverance during those trials is what makes us complete, we see those very two things come together in the story of Abraham: actions that complete his faith.

Back to page 81. Is your book falling open to that page, yet?

Check out verse 23 this time. Put a heart around the the name that Abraham was given. In fact, God gave him this name.

> Perseverance completes faith by demonstrating the genuineness of faith.
>
> Richardson, 140

Why do you think Abraham was given that name? What about him caused him earn the name of "friend of God"?

FRIEND OF GOD
ISRAEL HOUGHTON
http://bit.ly/JustJamesFriendofGod

James is going to be very James-esque and expound further on this idea of friendship with God in chapter 4, so, for now, we're going to continue through this passage.

While verse 24 may sound like it's touting that works save, be assured it is not. Remember that James has repeatedly said that faith apart from works is dead because faith, pistis, spurs us to action. What James is reiterating is that faith and works go hand-in-hand. James and Paul, best buds that we imagine them to have been, would have firmly agreed that "...by works of the law no human being will be justified..." (Romans 3:20). However, they also both would have agreed that "...by grace you have been saved through faith. And this is not your own doing; it is the gift of God, not a result of works, so that no one may boast" (Ephesians 2:8-10).

Let's take chapel with kids as an example. If we were preparing to teach the story of David and Bathsheba, a story that holds very vital truths for all ages, we would prepare VERY differently for an elementary chapel than we would for a high school chapel. The subject matter wouldn't be changing as much as the angle. We would be differentiating in order to meet the maturity level and the current struggles of the audience.

Paul and James are doing **just** that. In Romans, Paul's audience is dealing with much different questions than the questions of the people of Ephesus that he deals with in Ephesians. James's audience is also different, so their angles and answers match their audience while their message stays the same.

STUDYING THE BIBLE TIP

Remembering the original intended audience is always vital when studying Scripture. The angle from which the author comes will be different based on the audience's struggles and needs.

Faith that works

We know by now you know what we're gonna say....😌 go ahead and re-read James 2.

James 2 may be wrapping up, but James is not finished with the point he was making in verses 14-26.

Head back to page 81.

Put brackets around the very first prepositional phrase in verse 25. (In case you need a quick English course refresher, 🤓 prepositions show the POSITION of things - nouns specifically. So, they're words like on, against, under, etc.)

You see, James isn't about to embark upon yet another point. Quite the contrast, he's about to embark on yet another example of his current point. And while many of us would recognize and know a lot about his example from yesterday - Abraham - today's example might be a bit more obscure or fuzzy for us - Rahab. If you are unfamiliar with her story or if it's been a while since you've read her story, turn to Joshua 2:1-24 and take a minute to read it.

Before we dive into her story a bit more and unpack why James would use her as an example, let's look at a chart that Platt includes in his commentary on James (61).

ABRAHAM	RAHAB
▶ the patriarch of the Jewish people	▶ a prostitute in the middle of a Gentile nation
▶ the friend of God	▶ living in the middle of the enemies of God
▶ a great leader	▶ a common citizen
▶ at the top of the social order	▶ at the bottom of the social order

To use Platt's words again, Rahab was a recipient of God's "scandalous grace"...as are we (61). In the eyes of her culture - and even in ours - she was a low one on the totem pole. A prostitute. Not someone that we would pick out for God to use, right? Wrong.

Turn to Matthew 1. Genealogies aren't exactly the most riveting part of Scripture, but they hold some fun facts and connections that we might otherwise miss.

Look at verse 5. Whose name do you see?

If you follow those verses and get your family tree brain in gear, you will see that Rahab is actually Ruth's mother-in-law (Platt, 61). What?!?!?! 😮 And then, if you back out even further, you see that Matthew 1 is actually unpacking Jesus' genealogy. That means Rahab was a part of Jesus' family line! Scandalous grace, indeed!

This story tells us a lot about faith and a lot about our Savior. Rahab was currently living in sin at the time the spies came across her path as far as we can tell, but we also know that she knew about the One True God. How do we know that? Her actions.

When she encountered the spies, she had a choice to make: she could tell the king of Jericho where they were or she could hide them to protect them. She knew to Whom these men belonged, so she made the actionable choice to hide them and send them off when it was safe. Rahab made a bold choice - one that could have caused her entire family to be killed, one that could have caused her own death. But because she believed God, she was willing to obey what she knew He would want. She put herself on the line at the risk of death. Her faith was put into action.

James isn't the only one who mentions these two as heroes of the faith. The book of Hebrews mentions them as well. Hebrews is the book that sits right in front of James. Flip back a few pages to Hebrews 11 and read verses 17-22 and 31.

You know what we love about seeing the list in Hebrews? It shows that Abraham's one action of faith had an impact on so many other people. Abraham's choice to obey in faith impacted Isaac. Isaac learned faith from his father and, in turn, he obeyed in faith and impacted Jacob and Esau. Jacob then acted in faith and on and on down the line it went.

When we step out in faith, it doesn't **just** affect us, it affects generations of God's people. When in the midst of a trial God chooses to test our steadfastness, our perseverance, our choice doesn't **just** matter for our sake, but for the sake of those around us and for the sake of those who will come behind us.

LET'S REFLECT ▶ ▶▶ ▶

Right now, where you are, are you willing to lay everything on the line like Rahab did? Even if it meant death for you and/or your family? Are you willing to be *that* obedient to Jesus?

James ends chapter 2 by repeating something that he has said many, many times **just** in verses 14-26 alone. Remember that we said when reading Scripture, when something is repeated, we should pay close attention to it.

Why don't you write that verse below.

Both Abraham and Rahab had operative faith. Their faith moved from verbal to operative the moment they put action to their words of belief.

Considering both stories, jot down some things that stood out to you from each and then decide which one you feel applies to you more right now.

ABRAHAM

RAHAB

HOW DOES THAT APPLY TO MY LIFE?

Warning: We are entering into a territory filled with briars and thorns, one that will leave you scratched up, bruised, and feeling a little - okay a lot - guilty. Please make sure you have put on your safety gear. Ahead: The Tongue.

But in all seriousness, this is gonna be painful, y'all!

Let's begin as we do - read James 3:1-12.

Feelin' the burn? the sting? the OUCH? Us, too!

James really hasn't minced words up to this point, but he really ain't mincin' them now! As we've watched him do many times up to now, he is going to pull out yet another point from chapter 1. He is going to expound greatly on 1:19: "...be quick to hear, slow to speak..." He is also going to tie that into 1:8 about the "double-minded man." So buckle up!

We might begin by first asking, "Why is James harping on words so much??" Well, quite honestly, it's because God the Father and Jesus make a big deal about words.

Remember how we said that the metanarrative of Scripture is always important to keep in mind as you study Scripture? This would be a time that it would behoove us greatly to connect the dots.

Turn to Genesis 1. What 3 words do you see repeated in verses 3, 6, 9, 11, 14, 20, and 24?

Y'all, if in the beginning, God SAID, words have been important since the beginning! God could have chosen ANY way in the world, literally, to create the world, yet He chose to speak it into existence. Yes, that shows HIS power, but even more than that, it shows the power of words.

If you look a little further down in Genesis 1, you'll see that God also used words to reveal more about Himself. Check out verses 26-27.

According to those verses, the Godhead SAID that they were going to make man in the image of God, *imago dei*. He used humans to give us a glimpse of Himself.

In verse 28, He reveals more about Himself and His purposes by telling the male and female he **just** created, Adam and Eve, what He wanted them to do in the Garden He gave them.

In Genesis 2, God speaks commands to Adam and Eve, using words yet again to communicate His purposes. Also, can we **just** stop a minute and consider how HUGE of a deal it is that the God of the Universe was speaking to them using human words? Such an example of humility and such an example of His desire for relationship with us.

We see clearly in Genesis 1-2 that words have the ability to create, to communicate, to build-up. Now, as in most cases, there's a flip side. Enter Genesis 3.

Turn to Genesis 3:1. Who is speaking now?

Sadly, he continues to speak such twisted lies in 3:4-5 as well...and he hasn't stopped since that day.

Words are so important: they can create and build or destroy and tear down. One is patterned after God while the other is patterned after Satan. What James does in chapter 3 is ask us to consider which we are following. **#didwehearyousayouch #wesaidit**

Let's head back to James.

Who is James 3:1 addressing?

While James is actually addressing teachers of the Bible, most likely within the context of a church, we can't rule ourselves out quite so fast **just** because we are not teaching the Bible in the church. As Platt reminds us, the Great Commission in Matthew 28:19-20 calls all believers to "make disciples of all nations" and teach them to heed what Jesus says in the Bible (74).

We also think of Deuteronomy 6:7 that tells parents to teach their children God's Word and His ways while they sit with them, walk with them, talk with them, etc. We see daily, moment-by-moment teaching taking place here as well...teaching of the Bible.

Why do you think that those who teach are held to a higher standard?

Just like we are held to standards in our classrooms, teachers of the Bible need accountability as well. A good teacher doesn't walk into a classroom having no idea what she's teaching that day. A good teacher not only plans, but studies to ensure that she knows her material well and has a solid plan of how to teach that material to her students.

Just as a teacher who remains in a grade level for years gains experiential knowledge, so a teacher of the Word also gains knowledge and depth of understanding that they didn't have at first. In both cases, however, the teachers need that accountability.

Just like a good teacher would seek to gain an answer to a question she did not know for an inquiring student, so a good teacher of the Word studies to answer a question correctly rather than answering "on the fly," so to speak.

Teaching God's Word is certainly not an easy job. We must be studiers, diligent readers of God's Word. Because the Bible contains the Truth - the very Truth that helps us to find eternal life or eternal damnation - the judgment for those who teach it is rightfully more strict.

In James 3:2, it's almost like James wants to make sure these teachers know that perfection isn't possible. I mean, after all, he is a teacher of the Word, and he knows well that he is not perfect. So, here, he reiterates what he already said in 2:10.

In your own words, what is his reminder to these teachers - and us in general?

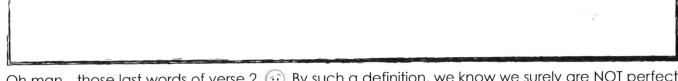

Oh man...those last words of verse 2. 😐 By such a definition, we know we surely are NOT perfect. You?

James is getting a bit **#punny** here. He uses the idea of "bridling" the tongue to introduce one of several analogies. The first one: a horse and its bridle.

Let's let you be the teacher here: teach yo'self! 😜 In the box beside the picture, explain James's analogy that matches each picture.

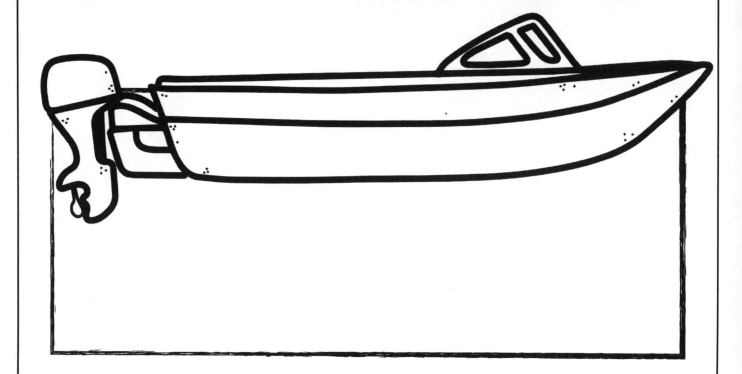

DAY 4 >>

So what's the point of all of these analogies? Well, to paint a very vivid picture about our tongues: they are powerful! As Proverbs 18:21 says, "Death and life are in the power of the tongue..." We have the choice - the very weighted choice! - of how we use that powerful tongue of ours.

Remember back to James 1:26? James warned us way back then. He said, "If anyone thinks he is religious and does not bridle his tongue but deceives his heart, this person't religion is worthless." **#ouchagain**

Chapter 2 was all about saying we had faith, yet not having the actions to back up that faith. Chapter 3 continues with a similar idea only about the tongue. James is in essence asking, "How do you claim to have faith in Jesus, yet you can't get control of your tongue?"

As John Gill said in his commentary on this passage, "...fire [is] very useful in its place...but [must be] watched and kept." Fire left unwatched and untended is dangerous. Mixed with the right conditions, it can cause a world of trouble.

Words used well can build up and encourage. Words left unwatched and untended are dangerous. Mixed with the right conditions, they, too, can cause a world of trouble.

So, the question would be: how do we tame our tongues? How can we fix our words? James is going to help us with that tomorrow.

LET'S DIG DEEPER > >>>

We know that today has been pretty painful. Why don't we end today by searching to see what Scripture has to say about the tongue. Use Google or biblestudytools.com or blueletterbible.org or the You Version app - whatever floats your boat. **#nopunintended** Write your favorites below.

Y'all ready for another day on the tongue??? 😄

James isn't letting us off that topic for quite a while yet, so settle in and re-read James 3:1-12.

We looked at James's analogies yesterday. They were quite vivid and convicting. In verse 6, James draws these analogies together and makes some startling statements. He tells us that "the tongue is a fire." Remember the fire from yesterday...this is no compliment! He says that the tongue "stain[s] the whole body." At the end of verse 6, he includes one of the most startling statements: the tongue is "set on fire by hell." **#yikes**

We don't know about you, but it seems to us that James wants us to get the fact that our tongues can do a lot of damage.

Remember back to Genesis 3? Do you remember who was talking?

The very first one to misuse the tongue was Satan. So when we are using words that destroy, according to Scripture, we are using words that have been "set on fire by hell." Y'all...we can't. If that doesn't get you in your core like it does us...

James goes on in verse 7 to say that every wild creature imaginable can be tamed, or so it seems, yet we can't seem to tame the tongue. The end of verse 7 almost makes the tongue take on a personality of its own, as though it came to life: "It is a restless evil, full of deadly poison." And doesn't it sometimes feel like that? You hear words coming out that you know shouldn't come out, but you're not quite sure where they're coming from or how to stop them! Our goal today is to figure out how to stop that "restless evil."

Before we get to the answer, let's continue on through our passage as James begins to expound on an idea he first introduced in 1:8: the double-minded man.

In James 3:9, what does James say we do with our tongues?

Do you hear the double-mindedness? It's like we shift back and forth between faith and hypocrisy according to James. And remember what he said in chapter 1: the double-minded should expect nothing from the Lord. **#hardpilltoswallow**

Do you remember James's definition of pure religion? James 1:27 taught us that pure religion was "to keep oneself unstained from the world." By jumping back and forth between faith and hypocrisy, blessing our Father and cursing those made in His image, we are not exhibiting a life unstained by the world.

James mentions two more analogies. (By the way, James knew - as did Jesus - that our brains love a good visual. So how did he teach? With visuals. **#goodteacher**)

What two analogies does he use for our tongues now in verses 11-12?

Okay...story time from Aesop's Fables:

A long time ago a Man met a Satyr in the forest and succeeded in making friends with him. The two soon became the best of comrades, living together in the Man's hut. But one cold winter evening, as they were walking homeward, the Satyr saw the Man blow on his fingers.

"Why do you do that?" asked the Satyr.

"To warm my hands," the Man replied.

When they reached home the Man prepared two bowls of porridge. These he placed steaming hot on the table, and the comrades sat down very cheerfully to enjoy the meal. But much to the Satyr's surprise, the Man began to blow into his bowl of porridge.

"Why do you do that?" he asked.

"To cool my porridge," replied the Man.

The Satyr sprang hurriedly to his feet and made for the door.

"Goodby," he said, "I've seen enough. A fellow that blows hot and cold in the same breath cannot be friends with me!"

Moral
The man who talks for both sides is not to be trusted by either.

DAY 5 ▶▶ DOUBLE TROUBLE

Aesop's fable teaches the very same lesson that James was teaching. It "ought not be so" that we speak out of both sides of our mouth.

As one commentator said, the spring analogy represents our mouths while the fig tree analogy represents our hearts.

Just as a spring cannot pour out both fresh and salt water, neither should our mouths pour out blessing and cursing, yet our mouths often do, don't they?

Just as a fig tree can't bear olives or a grapevine produce figs, neither should our mouths be able to produce blessing and cursing from the same heart that claims to love God, yet our mouths often do, don't they?

So, let's get back to our initial question that we introduced at the end of yesterday: how do we fix our words? What can we do about our tongue? The answer lies in our hearts, not our tongue. Even Jesus said this. Luke 6:45 says that "...out of the abundance of the heart he [or she] speaks." That means that when we have a words problem, we have a heart problem.

Why don't we look at some examples. Let's use our equation from earlier this week. We've given you two examples. You try your hand at the third one.

$$\frac{\text{Stated Belief} + \text{Actual Actions}}{\text{Actual Belief}}$$

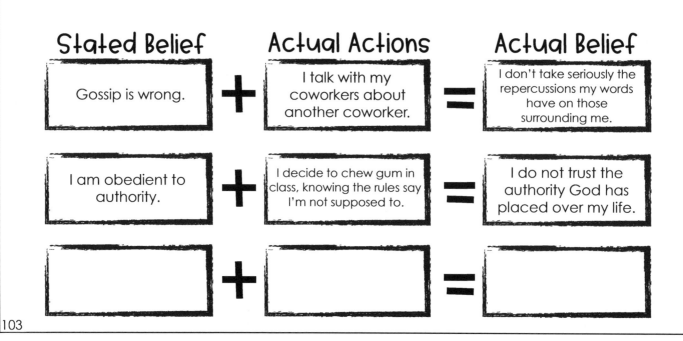

Stated Belief		Actual Actions		Actual Belief
Gossip is wrong.	**+**	I talk with my coworkers about another coworker.	**=**	I don't take seriously the repercussions my words have on those surrounding me.
I am obedient to authority.	**+**	I decide to chew gum in class, knowing the rules say I'm not supposed to.	**=**	I do not trust the authority God has placed over my life.
	+		**=**	

DAY 5 ▶▶ DOUBLE TROUBLE

We can see when we take a minute to reflect that when our actions don't match our stated beliefs, they really weren't true beliefs at all because "out of the abundance of our hearts, our mouths speak." Sounds an awful lot like what James was teaching even in chapter 2: our actions show our beliefs better than our words!

However, the reversal is true as well: our words will eventually become our actions - whether good or bad. What we say has a way of seeping into our hearts even if at first we didn't believe our own words. For example, if I tell myself I'm stupid enough times, eventually, I'm going to internalize that and believe it. On the flip side, if I tell myself I'm made in God's image enough times, that, too, will be internalized in my heart. The question is: what kind of words am I internalizing?

Words are powerful whether they're words that we speak to others, about others, to ourselves, or about ourselves. They can be patterned after God's Words as we saw in Genesis 1-2, or they can be patterned after Satan's words as we saw in Genesis 3. That is the very picture James **just** painted for us. He's going to go on to further unpack what characteristics each category of words have: heavenly or earthly, but his picture is pretty clear - our words need to match what we say we believe, which means our hearts must be shaped by God and His Word.

If we have a word problem, we have a heart problem. If we have a heart problem, we need more Jesus. If we need more Jesus, we need more of His Word in our hearts, so that He can transform us into His likeness.

LET'S APPLY ▶ ≫≫≫

Take a few minutes to think about ways that you can use your words to further the Gospel.

WEEK 5 >> VIDEO NOTES

Weekly videos can be found at http://bit.ly/JustJamesVideos

SCRIPTURE MEMORY: "But the wisdom from above is first pure then peaceable, gentle, open to reason, full of mercy and good fruits, impartial and sincere. And a harvest of righteousness is sown in peace by those who make peace." James 3:17-18

James focuses an awful lot on discipline...and rightfully so. If you think about the word Jesus used for His followers, *disciple*, both words share the same root. A disciple is one who is disciplined in ways that help him or her look more like Jesus.

Discipline, as every teacher knows, has a place within the classroom. While it may not be our favorite aspect of teaching, it is necessary and can bring forth some amazing fruit if done in the right way.

FROM BONNIE

Teaching elementary requires discipline for sure as we are helping to mold and shape little future adults. Consistency is absolutely key. Clear expectations are also key. What I try to keep in mind as I have discipline conversations with my littles is the heart. What I'm after is not **just** the symptom - the outward issue - but I want to help shape their little hearts for Jesus. Even in the public school system, it is possible to help shift their focus from self to others by teaching character traits like kindness and self-control.

When I have conversations with my littles, I want to point out the self-focused actions: bumping into my friend, taking toys from my friend, saying ugly and hurtful words to my friends. I want them to understand that a heart that is kind, a heart that is loving, a heart that loves Jesus pays attention to others before self. When I can help to shift their focus from self to others, discipline and growth is taking place. Their little hearts are being shaped in big ways.

FROM BETHANY

Dealing with discipline in the upper school world seems to grow increasingly difficult. The generation we are dealing with has an air of self-entitlement like none other. It is a generation who wants to take responsibility for nothing. Whether in the public or private school world, it is important for us to discipline well. (Discipline...not to be confused with punishment.)

When I have students who need discipline, I often pull them aside and discuss how their actions are setting a pattern for their entire life - because my goal is to help shape who they are and hopefully help them reflect Jesus. Because they are in the formative stages of their growth, whatever habits they form in middle and high school often follow them into the adult years. If I can get them to see how off-putting some of their forming habits would be in later years, it truly helps them to correct themselves before I have to use the school's consequence system to punish them for choices. However, I must be proactive, catching these behaviors before they've gone too far. My number one reminder to myself in these situations is two-fold: 1) I am dealing with children...children who are not fully developed mentally or physically or emotionally, and 2) Outside struggles often find their way inside my classroom as students bring in their personal struggles. If I can remember both of those things, I will discipline differently - in a manner that offers grace and room for failure while promoting growth and change.

We know that some of·you may find it odd that we ended the week in the middle of a chapter. And while that may seem odd, it's actually not too odd when we remember how Scripture was originally written. Remember that translators "chaptered" and "versed" the Bible, not the original writers. They did it more for clarity than anything else. So remember as we dive back into chapter 3 today that James's audience would've read this entire letter as one, not as 5 distinct chapters with verses.

To refresh your memory - and because we know that repetitive reading helps us in study - go ahead and read James 3 in its entirety.

Last week, we unpacked the analogies that James used for the tongue. We learned that the tongue can easily be fueled by hell, causing destruction, or by heaven, bringing healing. James is going to further unpack these two very opposite forces - heaven and hell - that can drive not only our tongues, but also our very lives.

Words that inform, heal, and do good are the marks of wisdom.
Matthew Henry

The first question in verse 13 - back to those rhetorical questions James loves oh-so-much - may make your brain jump back to chapter 1...and rightfully so. As we've noted several times, James used chapter 1 as his thesis. He is here again to unpack something he mentioned briefly in his thesis chapter.

Wisdom. A word that seems to elude much of our culture today...or at minimum, is misdefined by culture. How do you think our culture would define the word *wisdom*?

James said in chapter 1 verse 5 that if we lack wisdom, we can ask God for it, and He will give to all generously and without reproach. Ringing a bell? However, he went on to say in verse 6 that we must ask without wavering.

Well, James is ready to unpack what wisdom looks like. And he is going to do so by comparing and contrasting a friend of the world to a friend of God.

That phrase should also ring a bell. Do you remember who received that name, friend of God?

DAY 1 ▶▶ HEAVENLY WISDOM

Lest we think that James is not going to connect wisdom with actionable or operative faith, if we read the end of verse 13, we will see that the way we know we have true wisdom is how we live. Once again he reminds us that **just** as Abraham's actions, his works, proved his faith in God, so, too, his works proved that he was operating on the basis of heavenly wisdom.

Let's take a look at what that wisdom looks like so that we can evaluate whether we are operating as a friend of the world or as a friend of God.

Before we get too far into the descriptions of each, let's **just** go straight for the root because that will help us see these verses and these characteristics from a different perspective.

Look at verse 16. What is the root of the issue here?

When we can identify the root issue, we have a much better chance of fixing the problem.

We're all about defining today, but how would you define jealousy and selfish ambition?

JEALOUSY

SELFISH AMBITION

While jealousy and selfish ambition are the root of some not-so-great characteristics we are about to see characterizes a friend of the world, there is a root to one who is a friend of God as well. What godly root do you see in verse 18?

No two things could be farther apart than jealousy and selfishness and peace! We are either driven by one or the other. And it probably wouldn't take most of us long to self-diagnose and discover which has reign over us most often. **#anybodysayingouch**

Let's get our hands a little dirty...okay, metaphorically. No one is actually going to dig in any dirt here. 😛

Since we're talking about roots, let's check out the difference between heavenly wisdom and earthly wisdom via some good ol' plants.

On each plant, right the root that fits. Then, on or around the leaves, write the characteristics that fit each type of wisdom. Verses 15 & 17 will help you out.

Do you remember when we talked about the importance of words and how Satan has been trying to manipulate truth through words since the Fall in Genesis 3? Well, we're seeing the same kind of manipulation here.

If you felt like the word "demonic" was rather strong, that's because it is. James is being quite blunt here. Earthly wisdom finds its father in Satan himself. **Just** as the tongue can be set on fire by hell (verse 6), the same is true of this "wisdom."

If the root of this earthly wisdom is jealousy and selfish ambition, and if it all started back in Genesis 3, where might those roots have creeped up in the story of Adam and Eve and the Fall of Man? What was Satan's lie, in other words, about God? about themselves? about the world?

Thinking back over the last couple of chapters of James, we can see that selfishness brings death...**just** like the plant illustration. All of the negative examples James has used - favoritism, the tongue, judgment - they all are rooted in selfish ambition.

We can be sure that any time we are more focused on self than others, we are operating under earthly wisdom rather than heavenly wisdom.

Can you think of a time that you know you were operating under earthly wisdom? (No worries - if you don't want to write it, you don't have to do that, BUT we do encourage you to answer that within your own heart. Spiritual surgery still goin' on here!)

Can you identify some patterns in our world right now that would prove that our world and our culture often operates under earthly wisdom?

 Gaining more social media followers

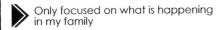 Only focused on what is happening in my family

On the flip side, we have heavenly wisdom whose root is peace. James's wording when talking about this kind of wisdom sounds an awful lot like Jesus and the Sermon on the Mount. Many commentators point this out, and we think it's worth noting.

Open your Bible to Matthew 5:1-12. Match each characteristic of heavenly wisdom to its Sermon on the Mount verse.

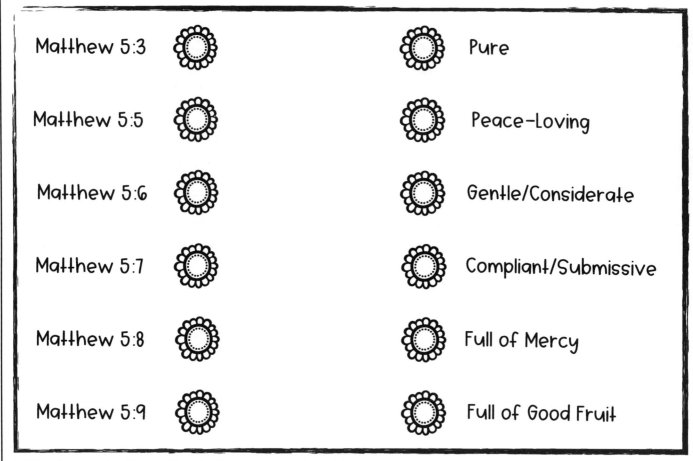

Matthew 5:3	Pure
Matthew 5:5	Peace-Loving
Matthew 5:6	Gentle/Considerate
Matthew 5:7	Compliant/Submissive
Matthew 5:8	Full of Mercy
Matthew 5:9	Full of Good Fruit

Is it **just** us or do things like that make you stand in awe of Scripture? When one passage speaks so clearly to another, the inspiration of God's Word stands out in all its glory!

Abraham is our picture from James of this type of wisdom. He was called "the friend of God." Why? Because he demonstrated trust and the use of heavenly wisdom. He had operative faith, not **just** verbal faith. And when operative faith is at work, it is operating with heavenly wisdom.

We can be sure that any time we are more focused on being a peacemaker, we are operating under heavenly wisdom rather than earthly wisdom.

Let us clarify: we didn't say peacekeeper...on purpose. We said peacemaker. There's a big difference in the two. In the language of Scripture, you'll always find peacemaker, soooo what does that mean? What's the difference?

Your turn first. What do you think the difference between being a peacemaker and a peacekeeper is?

PEACEKEEPER

PEACEMAKER

One who attempts to keep the peace is most often one who won't necessarily speak truth. They will do anything to keep the peace - whether that's a positive or a negative thing. **#notgood**

A peacemaker is one who seeks to bring peace where there is none.

So one keeps the peace - or whatever semblance of peace exists - often by not-so-great means. The other takes peace where it doesn't exist.

Do you think our culture values peacemaking or peacekeeping more? Explain.

Identify some areas in our culture where we try to be peacekeepers rather than peacemakers.

> Covering sin

> Tolerance over truth

>

According to James, and more importantly Jesus, heavenly wisdom is one that brings peace, not keeps peace. And where does true peace come from? The Truth - with a capital T...and that Truth with a capital T comes from the Bible.

DAY 1 ▶▶ HEAVENLY WISDOM

Let's do some more introspection...some more spiritual surgery on our own hearts. Where do you find yourself desiring **just** to keep the peace rather than be a peacemaker?

When we operate our lives using heavenly wisdom, there is a harvest, a reward. Verse 18 tells us that when we sow in peace, we will reap a "harvest of righteousness." Not immediately, but eventually, eternally.

Wisdom from above is so very different from what our world sees as wisdom. That often ill-defined word is defined so clearly and beautifully in James.

End today by spending a few moments asking God to help you operate with heavenly wisdom as opposed to worldly wisdom. You can write your prayer or simply spend a few minutes talking to Him now.

GIVER OF WISDOM,

Today, James continues his discussion of worldly wisdom versus heavenly wisdom in **#masterteacherstyle** He has defined the two types of wisdom, and now, it's time for a bit of personal application. Have you ever noticed that your students' buy-in increases when you can get them to apply a lesson personally? It's like teacher magic! 😍

Head to James 4 and read verses 1-5.

James wastes no time at all jumping right back into a rhetorical question that certainly would have captured their attention: "What causes quarrels and fights among you?" While this question, according to some commentators, actually alluded to cultural issues going on, James was also certainly pointing the finger right back at his audience.

As we've seen him do before, James asks questions only to give the answer he is looking for. What does he say is causing these quarrels and fights? (Hint: The answer is still in verse 1.)

The Greek word for "passions" is *hedone*. This word should sound familiar to some of you. We get our word hedonistic from this root.

Why don't you define hedonistic? A good ol' English dictionary will do.

Does that definition sound like our current culture or what? 😳

How many news stories, Instagram posts, Facebook posts, Tweets, etc. point to someone seeking his or her own pleasure at the risk of someone else's hurt, harm, abandonment, etc.? Can you think of at least one cultural example of this hedonistic lifestyle?

While this behavior seems common and perhaps even expected in the secular world, we must remember that James wasn't speaking to non-believers. He was speaking to believers. He was reminding them that going after the lusts of their hearts without even inviting God into the equation would inevitably lead to quarrels and fights. This sounds familiar...pretty sure James is hinting at chapter 2 verse 8 again: "...You shall love your neighbor as yourself..."

DAY 2 >> NOBODY LOVES ME LIKE YOU

When we are so focused on self and on self's desires, we are not focused on others and are certainly not setting out to love others as we love ourselves. In fact, James is about to unpack how detrimental and devastating this hedonistic way of living is.

Look at verse 2. What is the result of desiring something, yet not getting what we desire, according to James?

☐ ☐ ☐ ☐ ☐ ☐

While this sounds harsh, Jesus taught something very similar in His Sermon on the Mount. Let's head to Matthew 5:21-22.

Jesus equates murder with what? [_____]

It is interesting to note that James doesn't once say that these quarrels and fights spring up from hell or Satan. He points the finger back at our sinful desires, which take root in our sinful hearts. Never has there been a clearer picture of **just** how sinful we are.

This idea of anger goes all the way back to chapter 1 verse 19 again. James warned us to be "slow to anger" for this very reason. Godly anger is rare. We more often than not exhibit ungodly anger - anger that is rooted in bitterness and pride and self-seeking. When anger boils up enough, it spills over, and it burns anyone and everything in its path. Anger is destructive **just** like murder.

While James was most likely speaking metaphorically, we must recognize his warning as the severe warning that it is. Anger is destructive. Anger replaces rational thought, and we do things that we may not typically do in the heat of our anger. Oh Lord, help us to be "slow to anger!"

Look back at verse 2. Secondly, James says that we "fight and quarrel" because we what?

☐ ☐ ☐ ☐ ☐

Richardson puts it this way: "Whereas envy [that's our word, *hedone*] is willing to destroy in order to gain what belongs to another, coveting is willing to steal what is not one's own" (176).

Let's again turn our attention to our culture for this one: how does our culture spur us to covet, to want what someone else has that we do not?

[   ]

DAY 2 >> NOBODY LOVES ME LIKE YOU

We don't know about you, but we feel bombarded with covet-traps, so to speak. Everywhere we turn, we are faced with things, things, and more things. In fact, most of social media thrives on showing others all the things we have so others can want all the things we have! It's scary!

However, when our hearts are content - truly content - with what God has given us and where He has us, these covet-traps will fail. You see, at the root of coveting is distrust. Distrust of what or who? God. When we want something that someone else has to the point that it is eating us up and causing us to quarrel and fight with others because we are so discontent, we are saying to God, "What You've given me isn't enough. In fact, You've left out some good things that I need. I know better than You. And until You give me what I want, I'm going to throw a toddler-level temper tantrum." Does that hurt y'all to read as much as it hurts us? 😞 So very convicting!

At the end of verse 2, James tells us precisely why we don't have what we want. What does he say?

```



```

It's as though prayer never entered our minds, he says. We haven't asked. And, again, back to chapter 1, he already told us that God will give wisdom generously and without reproach to those who ask. The problem is, it isn't wisdom we want. And that's what James is about to say in verse 3.

> ³You ask and do not receive, because you ask wrongly,
>
> to spend it on your passions.

A good teacher anticipates her students' questions before they ask them. James has done that here. He can already hear someone saying, "But James, I DID pray." And he says, "Ah, but you prayed wrongly. Your selfishness was still at work in your prayer." Can't you see that student's face after such an answer? We know you've seen it before! 😮 It's the "How'd She Know??" face!

Above, bracket the part of verse 3 that shows us how James's audience wants to use what they've asked the Lord to give them. (Hint: **#englishnerdhint** 🤓 It's an infinitive phrase. An infinitive is to + a verb. An infinitive phrase is to + a verb + any words that go with that verb.)

How often is this us, too? How often do we pray about something, asking God to give us [fill in the blank], knowing full well that we have no intention of using it to help others, but rather we have full intention to use it on what suits our selfish desires? Too often to want to think about, huh?

According to James, what we need to watch is that our prayers don't become self-absorbed and self-focused. When we pray out of true faith, our prayers will be selfless because they'll be about God's will, not our will. We will want only what God wants to give us because it won't be about our agenda; it will be about what brings Him the most glory. "Our Father in heaven, hallowed be Your name. Your kingdom come, Your will be done, on earth as it is in heaven..." (Matthew 6:9-10)

Do you remember waaaaaaay back to the beginning of our study when we talked about the covenant between God and His people, Israel? James alludes to that covenant here. We have to read verse 4 with that covenant in mind, or this verse will be more confusing than clear.

Remember that much of the Bible is written in this covenant language: Jesus represents the Bridegroom, the Church (or His followers) represents His Bride. With that in mind, what marriage language comes into play in verse 4? **Just** one word will do...

[ ]

That's some strong language right there! Something important to note that many commentators point out - the fact that he uses the word *adulterous* shows that He is referring to believers. He isn't saying that these people were complete "friends of the world," but rather they were "unfaithful lovers" (Richardson, 178). This isn't the first place in Scripture that this language is used of God's wandering, unfaithful people. (If you'd like to see another example, read Ezekiel 16 or Hosea 1-3. Both are heartbreaking accounts of the unfaithfulness of God's people...and they become even more heartbreaking when we consider that we, too, have been unfaithful to Him.)

What we see in the latter part of verse 4 is the idea, once again, of the double-minded. According to James, what are we to God when we are a friend of the world?

[ ]

Adulterer, enemy of God...yikes! These are tough pills to swallow. How often do we try to live on both sides? We coax ourselves into believing that **just** a little bit of the world can't hurt us... right? 😬 But James says, wrong.

James says wrong because he says that as we allow our desires to guide us rather than the Spirit, we find ourselves in the constant battle of jealousy and selfish ambition. Sound familiar? Yep, chapter 3 verse 14. And the more we let those terrible, decaying, sin-filled roots take root, the more we place ourselves at enmity with God. And the more we are at enmity with God, the more we will find ourselves at enmity with others around us. Platt says it this way: "...hostility toward one another is really evidence of hostility toward God" (87).

Remember, at the root of this struggle is distrust. If we fully trusted God, our actions would exhibit that, and envy and covetousness are not evidence of trust. They're evidence of distrust and discontentedness.

Verse 5 helps us to understand why these harmful roots are so hurtful to God's heart.

> [5]Or do you suppose it is to no purpose that the Scripture says, "He yearns jealously over the spirit that he has made to dwell in us"?

Circle the word that tells us how God yearns for us.

While this word seems to be an odd one for God, it really isn't within the context of the covenant language. Go back to the marriage metaphor that is used for God and His people. In light of that context, what do you think it means that God yearns for us jealously?

When you are in a romantic relationship with someone, you, too, yearn jealously for that person. Yes, you want their affection, their devotion, their all. But you also want to see what is best for them play out in their life.

Think of this in the context of a parental relationship, too. It is only natural for a parent to want what is absolutely best for the child. That parent gave that child life, so that parent wants to see the child experience the best life he or she can experience.

Knowing that it was God Who breathed our very life into us (Genesis 2:7; Psalm 139), it should not be hard for us to conceive that He wants what is best for us. And He knows that friendship with the world is not going to achieve that kind of life for us. Friendship with the world is going to equate to anger and bitterness and self-seeking and conflict and the list could go on and on. He wants better for us. That's why He asks us to trust Him. That's why He asks us to be content with what He chooses to give us. He knows best what we need - yes, much better than we know.

James 1:17 told us that "every good gift and every perfect gift" comes from our Father, the One Who does not change, the One Who is constant. What if we trusted that the gifts He gave us were indeed perfect for us? Yes, even the ones that seem a bit painful in the moment. Even the ones that James says we should "count...joy" that have the scary label of "trial" on them. What if we trusted that the gifts He withheld from us weren't good for us? Yes, even the ones that seem to make the most sense for us to have in our limited perspective. What if we remembered that He is only good and always has our best interest at heart because "He yearns jealously" for us?

Let's end today by reminding ourselves that there is literally "Nobody Who Loves Me Like You Love Me, Jesus"! If you're struggling with this truth because of something that is going on in your life right now, why don't you take some time and ask God for the wisdom He promises to give. Ask from a humble heart, one that seeks to trust Him fully.

NOBODY LOVES ME LIKE YOU, JESUS
CHRIS TOMLIN

http://bit.ly/JustJamesNobodyLovesMeLikeYou

NOBODY LOVES ME LIKE YOU LOVE ME JESUS

Aren't you glad that the Bible doesn't only talk about our sin, never offering an antidote? We are so grateful that the antidote for our sin is crystal clear in Scripture!

James may have spoken some hard words over the past several verses, but today, he is going to offer us the antidote to our jealousy and selfish ambition.

Let's back up a bit today and read all of the verses that have discussed our problem so that we can fully appreciate the solution. Read James 3:13-18 through James 4:1-10.

Verse 6 is like the hinge that swings between the problem and the solution here. Doesn't that sound like **#teachertalk**?

Because the first 5 words of verse 6 are SO powerful, write them below.

```


```

Where would we be without that grace? Nowhere good. We know that much!

In verse 6, James reminds us of a vital truth that we see all throughout Scripture before he jumps into the solution for our problem.

> 6But He gives more grace. Therefore it says, "God opposes the proud, but gives grace to the humble."

Box the word, *therefore*. Underline or highlight the truth that follows it.

Remember, earlier, we said that when we see the word *therefore*, we must see what it is there for? Well, it's there to remind us of a truth that has been mentioned often in Scripture - both in word and example. We've actually already seen a story example of this truth in James. Do you recall where? Feel free to look back through chapters 1-4.

```


```

If you said the story of the rich man and the poor man who came into the assembly from chapter 2, you'd be correct. We specifically hear echoes of this truth in verse 5 of chapter 2.

> ⁶But He gives more grace. Therefore it says, "God opposes the proud, but gives grace to the humble."

From the beginning, we have seen that it is the humble, the lowly, the poor, that God has chosen to elevate. Why? Because a humble heart is a God-like heart.

Above, circle the word that tells us what God does to the proud.

The word for this opposition in the Greek is not pretty. The word is *antitassomai*. It means "to range in battle against." We aren't sure about you, but we know for ourselves - the last thing we want is for God to battle against us. No. No. And No! We want God battling WITH us, never AGAINST us!

So how do we make sure that we have Him with us rather than against us? We must live humbly. James is going to unpack a slew of imperatives, commands, that give us the solution to our problem of pride. And in case you haven't drawn this conclusion naturally, remember that under that root of pride is the jealousy and selfish ambition James mentioned in chapter 3.

> God is tirelessly on our side. He never falters in respect of our needs, he always has more grace for us...His resources are never at an end, his patience is never exhausted, his initiative never stops, his generosity knows no limit: he gives more grace.
> J.A. Motyer

If distrust and discontentment is at the root of our selfish desires, if our selfish desires lead us to becoming friends of the world rather than friends of God, then it is submission to God which will turn all of that upside down and get us right side up again. And under the heading of that submission, we will find eight imperatives that we must follow in order to get ourselves back on track.

RESIST THE DEVIL

You might think that the word for resist here would be the same as the word for oppose in verse 6, but actually, it isn't. The word in the Greek is *anthistemi*. It means "to take a stand against." This word stands in stark opposition to the command we **just** saw - "submit to God." Rather than resisting God, we are to resist the Devil.

Resisting him might beg the question: how do I know he's in the issue I'm dealing with? Well, James has let us know the key to that as well. Remember James 3:14-15? If fights and quarrels are happening among believers, the Devil is sure to be there because only worldly wisdom, demonic wisdom, would be the root of such quarrels.

Let's think of some areas we need to resist him. We've given you two. You try the third one.

- Resist him when you are tempted to lose your temper with that student who pushes your buttons daily.
- Resist him when you are tempted to speak selfishly to your coworker or boss.
- Resist him when you are tempted to _____

If we resist the devil, what will the devil do?

DRAW NEAR TO GOD

If sin draws us away from God, repentance will draw us back to Him. That is what James is commanding here. We must learn to repent. And, no, this will not be a one time thing. In fact, it may be a many-times-a-day thing, and that's okay...because as verse 6 reminds us "...He gives more grace."

If we draw near to God, what will God do?

CLEANSE YOUR HANDS

This command comes from a symbolic ritual the priests of the Old Testament had. They would wash their hands prior to tending to any sacrificial work. This symbolized the cleansing of the heart, the inside, which James's next imperative will require.

Psalm 24:4 tells us that the one who has "clean hands and a pure heart" is the one who can "ascend the hill of the LORD...[and] stand in His holy place."

Lest we think it is something of our doing that allows us to commune with God, let's see what John 13:8 and John 15:3 have to say.

Choose one of those verses and write it below.

PURIFY YOUR HEARTS

This command clearly connects back to chapter 1 of James. He says that it is the double-minded who are to purify their hearts. You know what that reiterates for us? Our mouth issues, our mind issues, all our issues go back to one place: the heart.

James connects this command with the last one to emphasize that the outside can't be cleaned while the inside is ignored - and vice versa. The inside must be cleaned as well as the outside. What's inside is eventually going to come out, and what's outside is eventually going to seep in.

Isn't this what James has been teaching all along? What we truly believe - truly, not **just** what our words say - is going to affect our actions. In other words, what's on the inside is going to make its way to the outside. Our faith, if indeed true, will show in our actions, our words, our desires.

BE WRETCHED AND MOURN AND WEEP

While this one sounds rather depressing, it would do us well to consider why James says what he says. As Platt says, "Those who live in friendship with the world do not see sin as a big deal" (90). James - and Jesus - would say that sin is a very big deal. Sin is the very thing that separates us from God, a holy and righteous God. If we are not weeping and mourning over our sin, then it is possible that we are not seeing our sin as we should: wretched and awful, deserving of hell.

Cornelius Platinga, a professor, theologian, and author, said that "...the shadow [of the proper view of our sin] has dimmed...Christians [once] hated sin, feared it, fled from it, grieved over it... Nowadays, the accusation *you have sinned* is often said with a grin, and with a tone that signals an inside joke. At one time, this accusation still had the power to jolt people" (Platt, 90).

Where in our culture or in your own world do you see sin being treated as though it were nothing?

Our sin should break our hearts. Our sin should cause us to be miserable, to mourn, to weep. Nothing in us should be okay with sin because it separates us from the very One we claim to love Who sent His Son to die for us - in place of us - because of our sin.

The second half of verse 9 tells us to turn our "laughter [into] mourning and [our] joy to gloom." James isn't suggesting a life void of joy and laughter. However, he is suggesting a life that takes sin seriously.

Can you think of a sin that at some point in your own life you have treated as nothing? Where you didn't mourn over it, but perhaps even went so far is to laugh about it, or maybe **just** ignored it?

HUMBLE YOURSELVES

James has come full circle. He began this section telling us to submit ourselves to God, and here we are again with the same idea.

This idea of humbling ourselves is so very opposite of the jealousy and selfish ambition, the distrust and discontentment that James has been highlighting over the past few verses. When we humble ourselves, we are saying that we do trust God. We trust that His ways are best. We trust that His gifts are best - both those given and those withheld. It is the humble heart that is the God-like heart.

If we humble ourselves, what will God do?

When was the last time you followed these steps? Submitted yourself to God...humbled yourself under His hand...mourned and wept over your sin? If you're like us, this isn't something we find ourselves acquainted with on a daily basis...though it should be a daily occurrence. Why won't we end today by spending time submitting ourselves to the One Who loves us most. If there is sin in your life that He is bringing to mind, confess that to Him. Mourn and weep over it. Let Him bring healing to the places that sin has broken.

COME AS YOU ARE
CHRIS TOMLIN

http://bit.ly/JustJamesComeAsYouAre

124

GOD WHO FORGIVES AND CLEANSES AND REDEEMS...

As a teacher, have you ever noticed how the content you teach builds on previously taught content? Of course you have! Every good teacher knows that students need solid foundational instruction because one concept builds upon another. For example, in Kindergarten, students learn letters and sounds so that they can begin to blend together those sounds and make words. As they learn to read those words, they can begin to write words together to make simple sentences. While learning the structure of writing begins in Kindergarten, it will follow them all the way to the high school English classroom. Although the content changes and deepens from year to year, it is building upon something that was previously taught. James is a good teacher, and so we see that the content he is teaching builds upon itself like building blocks.

This next passage serves as a bookend to the discussion about our tongues that he started in the beginning of chapter 3. Why don't you put in the extra work today and go all the way back to James 3 and read through James chapter 4 verse 12.

Yesterday, we ended our day studying a six-letter action word in James 4:10. Re-read that verse. What are we called to do before the Lord? (Hint: The six-letter word goes in the first box.)

Our humility affects our speech and attitude towards others. In the past weeks, we have painstakingly learned the power of our speech. Think back over what you have learned about worldly speech, and below, write ways that our speech affects those around us.

How does our speech affect our relationship with God?

In our study earlier this week, James referred to us as what kind of people? (Hint: Look at verse 4.)

Today, we will notice a shift in how James refers to his audience. Can you find that shift in the text? Look at verse 11. What does he call his readers?

The spiritual adultery refers to our relationship with God and concerns our need for repentance and choosing to love and obey God rightly. If we repent of the spiritual adultery, then that will change our relationship with our brothers and sisters around us. Is your teacher brain shouting CAUSE AND EFFECT!?!?  Our relationship with God will affect our relationship with those God has placed around us. James is shifting us from the discussion of our relationship with God to thinking about how that relationship affects those around us - our brothers and sisters.

> ¹¹Do not speak evil against one another, brothers. The one who speaks against a
>
> brother or judges his brother, speaks evil against the law. But if you judge the law,
>
> you are not a doer of the law but a judge. ¹²There is only one lawgiver and judge,
>
> he who is able to save and to destroy. But who are you to judge your neighbor?

The word *speak* is used three times in verse 11. We have learned that when something is repeated in biblical text, we should pay attention to the repetition. Go ahead and underline the word *speak* in your favorite color.

Now, in the verses above, place brackets around what we are speaking to our brothers and sisters.

In the Greek, this word, *speak*, is translated as *katalaleo*, which means "to speak against." But of the three times this word is mentioned, another translation of this verb is "slander." When we speak against someone, we criticize them. Slander is an all out attack on someone's character that would cause damage to a person's reputation. When we gossip or slander or cast judgment against someone, we are holding people to our standard, not God's standard. We belittle the judgment of God and place ourselves in a higher authority position than the Creator of the Universe. Does that statement make you say ouch?!?! It certainly made us squirm. James ain't mincin' his words!

Unfortunately, due to our sinful nature, we have all found ourselves on the giving and receiving end of gossip, slander, and judgment. When this dangerous trio finds its way into a classroom, school, or home, it will annihilate any sense of community, unity, or brotherhood/sisterhood.

Can you think of a time in your life where this dangerous trio - gossip, slander, judgment - caused chaos in your life or school workplace? Write about that time below. If you are uncomfortable writing about it, list the damage that it caused: broken relationships, loss of a job, loss of marriage, etc.

Read the passage below again. Mark the repetition found in verse 11 in the same way you did on the previous page. Circle the word that tells us how many lawgivers and judges there are.

> ¹¹Do not speak evil against one another, brothers. The one who speaks against a brother or judges his brother, speaks evil against the law. But if you judge the law, you are not a doer of the law but a judge. ¹² There is only one lawgiver and judge, he who is able to save and to destroy. But who are you to judge your neighbor?

How many times in the classroom do we find ourselves in dilemmas where we have 15 different lawgivers and judges when **#situations** arise? Everyone has his or her own opinion and viewpoint of how it all went down. In our limited knowledge of certain personalities and proclivities, we are left to be the judge presiding over the situations in our classroom. We don't know about you, but we have often found ourselves in situations where we feel insufficient in making a **#ruling** because of our lack of knowledge. Teachers are not all-knowing. Teachers are not all-wise. Teachers can not see all the things. Teachers can't always see the bigger picture.

The same can be true of situations that happen in our lives outside of the classroom. Let's chew on this scenario: a student gets in trouble in your classroom, and you send them to the office. Said student goes to talk to an administrator, and the student is sent right back to the classroom. Admin does not make the call that you think should have been made in that situation. You gossip to your neighbor teacher about the decision admin made. You even push it as far as slander by saying that they don't have the backbone to deal with the student or their parents. Sound familiar?

Here's the thing - in that situation when we gossip, we assert that we are all-knowing and that admin should handle situations in ways that we deem appropriate. Admins are not all-knowing, and they do make decisions that are wrong sometimes, but if we get in the practice of judging them for their decisions, we are doing the very thing about which James warns his readers. We as teachers realize that we have limited knowledge in classroom situations. We also need to realize that we are limited in our knowledge in situations that arise outside of our classrooms. We must seek the One who *is* the All-Knowing and All-Wise Righteous Judge. He is the only ONE who is deemed Judge. The presence of sin in our life means that we are automatically deemed insufficient to judge someone for his or her actions. We fall short of the mark that only the righteous Judge fulfills.

We often joke with each other when different situations arise at school that we should **#stayinyalane** Another class misbehaving? **#stayinyalane** Another teacher not doing his or her job? **#stayinyalane**

> Judging is an act that only the all-seeing, all-knowing God can perform. Only God, who knows the secrets of the heart, can judge that heart. Only God, who see what is done in secret, can judge these things long before they come to light.
> Richardson (194-195)

When it comes to matters of judging someone and his or her heart, we should remind ourselves to **#stayinyalane** and **#knowyourrole.** It is not in our authority to act as God. When we judge someone, we are placing ourselves in a role that is not ours. We need the very same mercy and grace as the one who we judge. The sin of slander cuts so deep that it not only hurts the people involved, but it is offensive to God Himself. We are not the final judge of someone's heart. That is God's job, not ours.

We have discussed what our role as a child of God is NOT. Let's stop and contemplate what our role is as a child of God. What do we have authority to do? In order to answer that question, we are going to send you to two different passages. Read both passages and come back and write what is our ultimate calling in life.

MATTHEW 28:19-20

COLOSSIANS 3:12-13 (HINT: THE ANSWER IS FOUND IN VERSE 13.)

DAY 4 ▶▶ KNOW YOUR ROLE

We, as believers, are called to preach and teach the good news of the Gospel message and make disciples. We are also commanded to forgive others who have sinned against us personally.

Let's close our day by reflecting on who the Righteous Judge is and our role as His children. If you have recently been in a situation where you have acted as the judge, spend some time confessing that sin and asking God to help you focus on the Ultimate Judge.

RIGHTEOUS JUDGE,

Raise your hand if you are a planner. 😊 Many teachers are natural-born planners. We certainly can't walk into a classroom without a plan for the day. We spend a large part of our time planning our days, weeks, months, and even the year to come. In fact, many of us know exactly what we will be teaching long before the school year has even begun. Survival depends on our planning.

We guess that many of you have tried to plan where you will teach, what grade level you will teach, and what path your career will take over the coming years. **#thatplanninglife** We have two questions for you: how many of your past plans unfolded **just** like you planned and how many failed? If you try to say that all of your plans are successful, then we would say that you **just** have not lived enough of your life yet. 😖 We spend much of our life hopping from one plan to the next trying to discover which path for our life is the best. Is that truly the way God intended for us to live our lives? We will spend the rest of today unpacking the answer to that question.

Go ahead and read James 4:1-17.

James 4:13 focuses on this businessman who travels and trades for a profit. This would have been common in the first century. The businessman who is described in this passage reminds us very much of our own culture today. He was focused on *his* plan for *his* life that would bring him wealth and prosperity. He possessed a worldly mindset, not a heavenly mindset.

How might this businessman be similar to our culture today?

Oh sweet teacher friend, we have a problem. We often get overtaken by the things of this world, and we forget our purpose is to live for the things of heaven. God does not have a problem with our planning, but the problem occurs when the planning is focused on our material profit. In fact, we would argue that God Himself is a planner. Woven throughout the entire Biblical story are smaller stories that are intricate and detailed, showing God's planning character. James warns his readers about making plans for the next year when they don't even know if they will have breath tomorrow.

We think that it would benefit you to write verse 14. On the next page, write the verse, and then, circle the word that describes us.

JAMES 4:14

Everything that we do and accomplish here on this earth is under the will of God. We shouldn't be arrogant to think that we have the ultimate power over the things we accomplish. **Just** because we give all the credit to God for our accomplishments doesn't mean that we are allowed to become lackadaisical in our life pursuits. James would shout at you, "NO!" Remember what he told us to be in James 1:22? Why don't you flip back and read that verse again.

Use the knowledge that you have gained thus far in this study and apply it to this passage today. What do you think James was telling his readers about the kinds of plans they should work towards in their lives?

Did your answer consist of something that would be kingdom focused? If it did, you are exactly right. James wants us to be an active people while also being completely dependent on God. Yet again, James is shouting a warning of becoming consumed with the things of this world.

The desires of this world can creep into our lives so quickly, and before we realize what is happening, it's stealthy ninja-like appearance overtakes our thoughts, decisions, and desires. We have this keeping up with the Jones' attitude. Soon, we will realize that the desires of this world are fleeting and temporary. We lose focus on what our real priorities and plans should be.

On the next page, take some time to jot down some areas of your life where the world might be creeping in on your desires and plans.

[blank box]

Let us speak to your hearts for **just** a minute…we as a people tend to live our lives waiting on the next moment. Do any of these scenarios sound familiar to you?

▶ I am single, and I can't wait until I find my future husband. Once I do, my *real* life can begin.

▶ I am married, and once we have children, our family will be complete.

▶ I will teach this school year in this *okay* district, but next year my goal is the better school district.

▶ **Just** one more year teaching this grade level, but next year, I will get my favorite grade level.

▶ My family and I will live in this house for now, but the ultimate goal is to live in a larger, nicer, and more updated house.

▶ Next year, I am going to live healthier and read my Bible more. I will serve more in my church next year when my life is more calm.

Why don't you try coming up with a scenario?

▶ [blank box]

Living life for the next moment ignores God's plan for your life right now. We aren't promised tomorrow. In fact, verse 14 tells us that our life is like a mist that is here only for a little time and then vanishes. God has a plan for each and every moment we experience in our lives. Don't spend your life wishing and waiting on what is around the corner because you will one day turn around and realize that your life has quickly passed you by without the recognition of what God has taught you through small moments of your life. We need to live our lives not wasting them on things of this world, but rather working to accomplish things that are kingdom focused.

What are some kingdom focused things that will make us "doers of the word?"

JAMES 4:17 ▶ ▶▶▶

James hits us with a one two punch at the end of this section by reminding us that if we know what is good and choose to ignore it that is a sin. This points back to Week 3 with the sins of commission and omission.

Sins of omission are quite serious and often overlooked. We tend to focus on the things that God tells us **not to do** and ignore His commands of what He has asked us **to do** in our lives. Even worse, we know His commands and blatantly ignore them because culture dictates something else. We bank on God's forgiveness and live our lives in the way we want.

In Week 3, we reflected on certain areas that are common for sins of omission. But today, let's spend some time today asking God to forgive us of our sins of commission and omission. We're really good at confessing the commission sins, so let's not be too quick to overlook any of the omission sins God brings to mind. After our time of prayer, let's jot down some areas in our life where we have been omitting what God has asked us to do in His Word. Let's make a plan to follow God's Word and be obedient to what He has asked of us.

SINS OF OMISSION

MY PLAN

WEEK 6 ▶▶ VIDEO NOTES

Weekly videos can be found at http://bit.ly/JustJamesVideos

SCRIPTURE MEMORY: "You also, be patient. Establish your hearts, for the coming of the Lord is at hand." James 5:8

If you have been a teacher for any length of time, you have inevitably dealt with **#thatclass** or **#thatstudent** 😬 We all know the kind: hard to get along with, hard to control, full of liars or gaslighters, hard to please...the list could go on and on. There are times - quite a few if we're honest - that we **just** wonder **#whyme**. There are days we want to call it quits with teaching because of these types of people. So, what do we do when we're given **#thatclass**? What do we do when we have to deal with **#thatstudent** or **#thatparent** or even **#thatadmin**?

FROM BONNIE AND BETHANY

James has not shied away from talking about tough trials and difficult people. In fact, he opened his letter with "...count it all joy...when you meet trials of various kinds..." Well, we sometimes meet these trials in the form of people within the walls of our school, and maybe even closer, within the walls of our classroom. James would tell us, too, to "count it all joy..." But that's so much easier said than done, isn't it? 🙁

One of the easiest things to want to do when we encounter tough classes or tough people is to remove any "extras." No games for y'all. No goody bags for y'all. No extra recess for y'all. When in reality, that's not how James would advise us to deal with it at all.

James reminded us when talking about dealing with the poor - the orphans and the widows - that getting in the midst of their affliction would be tough. And let's be real, affliction can make people act tough. They put up walls because they've been wounded before and don't want to be wounded again.

Let's step inside the shoes of a tough student: perhaps this student comes from a rough home - a home that barely survives financially, a home that is missing peace, a home void of one parent or the other. Perhaps this student has been called stupid his or her whole life - by friends, by teachers, by family. Perhaps this student is painfully shy. Perhaps this student is starving for attention. Perhaps this student has been bullied. So many possibilities.

Let's step inside the shoes of a tough class: we tend to find that tough classes are controlled by a tough student. Usually that student has sway over most of the other students. However, the same above reasons could explain that student's behavior.

While it's not easy to hear this when we're facing these tough ones, God has hand-selected our students, their parents, and our admin, knowing that either they need something we have to offer, we need something they have to offer...or maybe a bit of both.

Practically speaking, we need to spend a great amount of time in prayer for these students, parents, or admin. We also need to spend a great amount of time with them. The more interest we show in their world, their likes, their opinions, the more likely they'll be to let us in. Bethany likes to call this head-to-head combat. There are **just** times when we're going to have to gear up for battle, but once we stand our ground a time or two and once we show them that we care about them for real, they'll back down. It may take a while, but the last thing they need is for one more person to give up on them. James would tell us to persevere because "...the testing of our faith produces steadfastness..." which will lead us to "be perfect and complete, lacking nothing." You see, if we remember that our Savior uses every part of our lives to help mold us to be more like Him, we will realize that even these tough students, parents, and administrators give us an opportunity to be doers of the Word. They offer us an opportunity to live out our faith through our works. After all, as cliche as it may sound, we may be the only Jesus they ever see.

Next time we are faced with **#thatclass** or **#thatstudent** or **#thatparent** or **#thatadministrator**, let's ask the Lord to help us to have the wisdom to know how to deal with them in ways that shout His love to them.

James is now bringing his letter to a close, but get ready! Because this ain't gonna be a smooth ride! This ending is rocky, blunt, fast-paced...it's almost like he decided that he needed to conclude but had 1001 more things to say. So buckle up!

Go ahead and read James 5:1-6.

Based on those 6 verses, how does this section of James seem to connect with 4:17?

A while back, Week 3 to be exact, we discussed the difference between sins of commission and sins of omission. While James has certainly dealt with both types, we see him revisit both here in one single example.

The main sin of omission James has dealt with up to this point came from James 1:27-2:1-7 when he discussed taking care of the poor. Here, in chapter 5, he revisits the subject of the poor versus the rich.

James is repeating some of his language from chapter 4, telling his audience - a slightly different audience than the rest of his letter - to "weep and howl" because of the sins they had committed.

So, who is James's audience now? (Hint: It's in verse 1.)

While James has been quick to repeat the phrase, "my brothers," throughout his book, he omits that here, which leads many commentators to believe that James is no longer talking to believers. So...why would he switch audiences in the middle of his letter? Great question!

What James is about to unpack is the consequences that the rich are going to suffer if they do not repent. These consequences are coming to them because of how they treated the poor, particularly those who worked for them. Who worked for them? Well, based on James's letter, we have every reason to believe that some of the very people James has been talking to throughout his letter, worked for these rich that he is now addressing.

His shift in audience may be because he thinks the rich will somehow happen upon this information, but even more likely, James wants his hearers to know that God is not overlooking this major trial that has been upon them - one of poverty because of the rich. He wants them to "count it all joy" because the Lord of Sabaoth has heard their cries. (More on that name of God later.)

Let's break these verses down as one commentator has: the misery of hoarding, the misery of wasting, and the misery of innocent blood.

▶ THE MISERY OF HOARDING

What has happened to the rich's riches? (verse 2)

What has happened to the rich's garments? (verse 2)

Do you recall the description of the rich man in chapter 2? Verse 2 told us that he had on "fine clothing." It is probably not coincidental, knowing James's style of writing, that he now talks to the rich and mentions their moth-eaten clothing. It serves as a warning against hoarding material things.

What has happened to the rich's gold and silver? (verse 3)

Interesting fact, in case you didn't know, gold can't corrode. So why would James include this statement about their gold corroding? Well, to prove his point, of course. The very thing the rich invested in and trust in, thinking that it would be their "salvation," so to speak, is the very thing that God will use to prove to them that riches won't last.

James seems to be echoing what 2 Timothy 3:1-5 warns believers to watch out for in the end days.

> ¹But understand this, that in the last days there will come times of difficulty. ²For people will be lovers of self, lovers of money, proud, arrogant, abusive, disobedient to their parents, ungrateful, unholy, ³heartless, unappeasable, slanderous, without self-control, brutal, not loving good, ⁴treacherous, reckless, swollen with conceit, lovers of pleasure rather than lovers of God, ⁵having the appearance of godliness, but denying its power. Avoid such people.

Underline anything above that seems to match the message of James 5:1-6.

▶THE MISERY OF WASTING

Verse 4 uses personification (giving human characteristics to a non-living object) to paint a more vivid picture for the rich. Artist or not (and in case you are wondering, we are stick people artists over here, y'all!😄), draw a picture that demonstrates what James is saying the wages, or money, that was meant for the workers is doing.

If the picture of money yelling at you to pay the workers their dues wasn't enough, surely the end of verse 4 would get you. Now, James says, "the cries of the harvesters have reached the ears of the Lord of Sabaoth."

You see, these rich, the "bosses," had withheld the money these poor laborers earned by working in their fields. The law was clear. According to Leviticus 19:13, when were the wages to be paid to the workers?

Many of the workers were highly dependent on this daily wage **just** for basic living necessities. They couldn't eat or find a place to lay their head without this money. Can you hear echoes of James's earlier cry to help the poor?

But remember, while James is addressing the rich, he is also reminding the poor that God is watching and will repay...which leads us to look a bit more closely at what the rich did and who heard the cries of these workers.

In verse 4, we see that the wages were "kept back" by the rich. The Greek word for this is *aposterero*. It literally means, "stolen." By not giving the workers their dues, the rich have literally stolen from them.

You know who's watching and listening as these poor cry out because they can't afford the necessities of life since the rich have stolen from them? The Lord of Sabaoth. While this name might not ring a bell for us, it would have for the Jews. Literally, this means "Lord of the Armies." They would have recognized this name of God as the "address [that] characterized God as the one who moves to deliver His people" (Richardson, 211).

Is it **just** us or is that a terrifying image? Not only is the Lord about to show up, but He's about to show up with His heavenly army in tow. A similar image was given in chapter 4 when James reminded the proud that God opposes them. The word for oppose was also a warfare word, meaning "to battle against." We don't know about you, but we never want to be on the receiving side of such a battle. 😳

You know what's scary? Our American culture has set themselves up for this very type of assault. We sit in the seat of luxury. We sit in the seat of wealth. Much like another place mentioned in Scripture...have you heard of Sodom and Gomorrah?

Turn to Ezekiel 16:49. What four reasons are we given for why Sodom and Gomorrah was destroyed?

Does that sound like America at all to you? That's scary and should be convicting to us, honestly.

Verse 5 tells us that the rich were living not only in luxury, but also in self-indulgence. This, too, is reminiscent of chapter 4 when James talked about desires that resulted in murder and covetousness that resulted in stealing. And BINGO! There's the connection!

The rich so desperately envied what others around them had - money, land, possessions galore - that they stole from the poor **just** so they could hoard more wealth. Wealth that would simply rot and end up being the evidence needed on the day of judgment to convict them of their sinful ways.

THE MISERY OF INNOCENT BLOOD

While murder seemed an arresting, extreme example in chapter 4, we see how it fits in chapter 5.

The poor, the harvesters, in chapter 5 were innocent. They had done nothing except work as they were hired to do. Yet, the rich withheld - stole - their wages so they could "fatten [their] hearts."

As we would expect, lack of wages would eventually lead to actual death. Whose fault would those deaths be? The rich. Had the rich paid the workers their earned money, they would have had enough to eat and to live. But they didn't. So the poor would eventually die simply because they were poor.

No wonder James has spent the better part of his letter teaching us to re-order our thinking... God's economy is upside down from ours:

- Trials should be counted as joy.
- Small things, like the tongue, have great power.
- God chooses the poor of this world to be rich in faith.

James has challenged us time and time again to consider that what seems normal and comfortable isn't always right. God's ways are often so different from what is natural because what is natural is so often sinful since we are sinful at our core.

James yet again quotes Jesus' own teaching here. In Matthew 12:7, Jesus said, "If you had known what these words mean, 'I desire mercy, not sacrifice,' you would not have condemned the innocent." James said it this way: "For judgment is without mercy to one who has shown no mercy" (2:13).

The rich will see their end. Their end will be one of destruction without mercy because they have been everything but merciful. James gives them one last chance: "Come now, you rich, weep and howl for the miseries that are coming upon you." You have a chance to repent still, James shouts to them...to us...but your time is quickly running out.

LET'S REFLECT

While we may not have left an employee unpaid, surely we have been guilty of living out of our luxury, our abundance, while knowing full well there were people around us struggling to make ends meet. It may feel like we've been here before because it's a message James keeps repeating - and that means it's an important one.

Take a look into your personal world right now. Do you know of someone - a coworker, a student's family, an administrator, a friend, a person on the street you pass daily - do you know someone who is struggling due to poverty? We all know at least one. How can you help? What abundance has the Lord given you that would allow you to meet a need of some sort for that person?

Remember what James 4:17 reminded us: "...whoever knows the right thing to do and fails to do it, for him it is sin."

Let's submit to God as James exhorted us. Let's humble ourselves before Him. Let's ask Him for wisdom to know who to help out of the abundance He has given us.

DAY 1 ▷▷   DO SOMETHING

As you listen to this song, ask God to show you where you are living like Sodom and Gomorrah, "overfed and unconcerned" (Platt, 98). Ask Him to open your eyes to those around you who need your help while changing your hearts to be like His, concerned for the least of these. Jot down some "light bulb moments" you have along the way that demonstrate what you can do for the least of these.

 DO SOMETHING
MATTHEW WEST

http://bit.ly/JustJamesDoSomething

DO SOMETHING

143

Good writers know that where you begin, you also should end. Essays, books, writings of any kind should be circular. However you hooked your reader, take them back there. Reinforce your original point. James is a good writer. We are about to see him circle right back around to his theme: patient endurance in the midst of suffering.

Go ahead and read James 5:1-11.

James is about to unpack three examples of patience. No matter the example, his message remains the same: "Count it all joy, my brothers, when you meet trials of various kinds, for you know that the testing of your faith produces steadfastness, And let steadfastness have its full effect, that you may be perfect and complete, lacking in nothing."

Before he unpacks each example, James reminds them that the end goal is to be patient until when? (Hint: The answer is in verse 7.)

When we live with the view of God's inevitable return in our mind's eye, we will be much better able to withstand the momentary sufferings here on earth.

▶▶THE FARMER

Since James was **just** addressing the misery of the poor laborers from whom the rich had stolen money, it is no surprise that his first example is the farmer, or the harvester.

James has been about the business of preaching dependence on the Lord from chapter 1. Here, he takes no different approach. He refers to the "early and late rains," with which the farmers would have been very familiar. But notice, he says that they "wait" for them. There is no fretting from the farmer. There is no anxiety about the rain coming or not coming. There is patient endurance, knowing that they must rely on the Lord for those rains.

It should be noted that this patient endurance is not a "do nothing" kind of waiting. The farmer would still need to take care of weeds and sowing and reaping when the time came for each, but the farmer also isn't daily fretting wondering if the Lord is going to keep His part of the deal.

Do you remember what James 3:17-18 said? Those verses hold two "farming" or "harvesting" words. Can you spot them?

Circle the one that you also see in James 5:7.

The Greek word for fruit is the same in both verses. Why does this matter? Well, because the lesson deepens a bit when we consider that they are the same. You see, when the Lord asks us to bear a trial, when He uses a trial to test our faith (James 1:3), what He's after is the fruit of heavenly wisdom. As the early and late rains of the trial comes, He's hoping that what will be reaped from such a harvest is purity, peace, gentleness, mercy, sincerity - the fruits of the wisdom James already discussed.

Think back to the last trial you endured. What kind of fruit was harvested from that trial?

James reminds them once again in verse 8 that they, too, **just** like the farmer, should strengthen their hearts, knowing that the Lord's coming was near. The unjust suffering they were enduring, the seemingly impossible trials, they were going to come to an end. The Lord of Sabaoth was coming to rescue His people.

▶▶THE JUDGE

Notice the switch in verse 9. While James's audience was turning their anger and frustration on the unjust bosses, they are now turning their anger on whom?

Oh man...we're back to the tongue! 😬 We **just** can't get away from that lethal thing!

One of the easiest things to do in the midst of tough times is turn our wicked tongues on each other. The very people who should be helping one another endure such difficult circumstances are often the very ones at each other's throats. This shouldn't be, James says!

Why do you think it is easy to turn against one another during times of hardship and trial?

James would quickly point us back to chapter 1 verse 19: "...let every person be quick to hear, slow to speak, slow to anger..." When we stop long enough to breathe and process who or what is the real issue, the real root, we will discover it is not our fellow believers walking alongside us. But wouldn't Satan have us think it is? The very thing he wants to do is knock us off the patient endurance train. He wants us entwined in so many knots with other believers that he can look at God and say, "See, I knew she wouldn't make it." We must resist him as James said in chapter 4 verse 7. He will flee if we will resist his attempts to entangle us in needless disputes and groanings with those believers around us.

James then mentions another level to this groaning issue in verse 9. He says that we shouldn't grumble against each other so that we may not be what?

[ ]

James has already discussed judging, but here, he seems to be reiterating something found in Matthew 7. Turn there and read verses 1-5.

In your own words, summarize what Matthew has recorded.

[ ]

Doesn't the message of Matthew 7 sound an awful lot like James 2:13? The way we judge others - and we judge based on our words and actions to others - is the way we will be judged. James reminds them here in chapter 5 that the Judge, Jesus, is standing at the door. He is ready to judge, and we do not want to have to answer for those careless words that we have spoken against a fellow believer (Matthew 12:36).

The prophets also knew such judging. Jeremiah and Ezekiel were two well-known prophets of Israel that James's audience would have known. Both endured some harsh judging words from God's people who simply did not like God's message that they were speaking. James refers back to these prophets as yet another example of patient endurance.

>> JOB

James has already mentioned Abraham and Rahab as examples of those who demonstrated their faith by their works. Now, he mentions another example not only of faith exhibited in works, but also of patient endurance in the midst of a trial.

 **DAY 2 >>**

PATIENT ENDURANCE

Job is a rather lengthy book, so we aren't going to ask you to pause and read all 42 chapters, but we are going to ask you to pause and watch this video about the book of Job, so we can make sure we have a good grasp on who Job was and what God's purpose with him was.

What are three take-aways from the video, three things that stuck out to you?

http://bit.ly/JustJamesJob

One of the first things we recognize from the book of Job and the example of Job is that trials aren't punishment. Job 2:3 would back this up. The Lord allowed Job to be tested by Satan to prove Job's integrity. Job questioned, yes, but Job endured steadfastly to the end.

Questioning doesn't always equate to a wrong heart. Richardson said it this way, "[Job is an exemplar in view of his great complaining]…because Job addressed his complaints properly to God and not against others." Job didn't allow his tongue to have free reign to attack those around him in the midst of his suffering. Rather, he turned his questions to the only One Who could answer them, God. Job did exactly what James told us we could do - he asked for wisdom from the One Who would give "generously to all without reproach." And for his asking, Job received a 30+ chapter discourse from God where God reminds Job that He is God, and He is only good.

In the end of verse 11, James calls his readers back to what they know: "…the Lord is compassionate and merciful." Job knew this, too. Job came out on the other side of his trial knowing that these traits of God were absolutely descriptive of who God had been to him in the midst of his trial. And while it may be hard to look through our trial-tinted glasses and see His compassion and mercy, certainly as we look back, we will see that He was indeed full of both.

LET'S END TODAY BY PAUSING AND ASKING OURSELVES: WHAT DID WE LEARN ABOUT GOD THROUGH THIS SECTION OF JAMES TODAY?

James is quickly coming to a close - as are we. However, be warned: his ending is going to require some theological big girl pants! 😄There's a lot to digest, so let's be about the job of digesting, not **just** ingesting. Let's don our critical thinking caps and gather all the things we've learned thus far and piece them together in these last few verses.

Go ahead and read James 5:1-18.

James has **just** unpacked examples of patience in suffering, connecting his readers right back to chapter 1 where he began this letter.

VERSE 12

Verse 12 almost seems like James forgot what he was talking about and went on a rabbit trail. However, if we look at this verse in light of the context of the entire letter, it doesn't seem so out of place. It goes back to the tongue yet again. James seems to be warning his readers that in the midst of enduring patiently, it is easy to be rash with your tongue. James would remind them that even in the midst of suffering, "faith that perseveres is trustworthy in speech. The words from our mouths should be so consistent and dependable that they guarantee reliability" (Platt, 100).

STUDYING THE BIBLE TIP

When you encounter a tough passage that you're struggling to understand and interpret, remember the whole of Scripture. Allow Scripture to help you interpret Scripture.

Basically, verse 12 is a tongue check point. Are you using your tongue rashly to make oaths with the very name that you claim to trust, or are you allowing your tongue to further back up your faith? Because ultimately, "one's conduct is largely determined by what one says" (Richardson, 228).

VERSES 13-14

James now is ready to assert that it is always an appropriate time for prayer. In these next few verses, he is going to expound on when we should pray, why we should pray, and how we should pray.

Verses 13-14 ask 3 rhetorical questions that give us a glimpse into when we should pray. Write those 3 questions times below.

We should pray when we are…

❶ _____

❷ _____

❸ _____

DAY 3 ▶▶ POWERFUL PRAYER

Why should we pray when we are suffering? Well, James has answered that for us already. James 1:5-6 reminds us that we can ask for wisdom when we meet various trials that **just** don't make sense to us...like Job from yesterday. Prayer during times of suffering will also keep our tongues in check, so we won't be tempted to grumble against one another (Richardson, 230).

Why should we pray when we are cheerful? Well, for one, in other places in Scripture, we are commanded to give thanks at all times and in all things. But also, prayer in the midst of cheerful times can also keep us from the boasting that James warned against in chapter 4.

Why should we pray when we are sick? James would have us connect this right back to chapter 1 where he discussed his theme of suffering and how we are to face suffering. Now, this is where our theological big girl pants are needed. James's emphasis here is on prayer for physical, bodily healing. Eight times - yes, 8 - in verses 13-18, we see words related to prayer: pray, praise, prayer, prayed. Any time Bethany teaches her students to locate theme, one of the keys to unlocking theme, she tells them, is looking for repeated words, phrases, and ideas. We must do the same with Scripture. So it is safe to say that James's theme here is prayer.

This isn't the first time he has mentioned prayer in his letter. Prayer has been something he has commanded prior to now as well. Why? Because James knows that prayer is powerful as we will see him say again in a minute.

In verse 14, James says that elders of the church should be called in to pray over and anoint one who is sick. We have to pause and consider the oil here for a moment. And we must do so in light of the rest of Scripture and in light of the letter of James. James has taught dependence on God throughout his entire letter. The metanarrative of Scripture also teaches us to rely fully on God. James has not switched his message here all of a sudden to teach that the oil that the elders use has some extra-spiritual power in it. No. James would agree that "the power for healing is not found in any oil but in the God who answers prayer" (Platt, 101). Oil was often used in the Old Testament to consecrate people and things. One example - David, when chosen to be king, was anointed with oil. Again, the oil had no special power, but it did represent David's consecration - he had been set apart by God, for God's purposes. The application of oil also did not heal David from his sins. If David believed that the oil had saved him and cleansed him, Psalm 51, his repentance song that he penned after committing adultery with Bathsheba, wouldn't need to be a thing, yet it is clear in that Psalm that he knew he desperately needed God, not an elder, to cleanse him and forgive him of his sin.

The very end of verse 14 echoes James's message of reliance on God, not the oil, and not the elders. What are the last 6 words of that verse?

James knew clearly and absolutely that only God has the power to cleanse and save. No human on earth, no substance on earth, can cleanse us. "...we all stumble in many ways..." James said in chapter 3, so none of us has the power to remove sin from another. None but Jesus.

VERSE 15

Verse 15 doesn't give our theological brains much of a break either.

According to James, what kind of prayer will save the one who is sick?

This statement brings back to memory James 4:3. James reminds his hearers that it is the prayer of faith and the prayer that keeps God's will, not our will, front and center, that has power. And herein lies the issue: when we pray for someone's healing, we often do so without considering God's will. It is easy to have our will in the forefront of our mind because as Job discovered, God's ways are so different than ours. His purpose behind the creatures He's made, His purpose behind nature, His purpose behind trials - all make but little sense to our finite human minds.

When we look at the metanarrative of Scripture, we see this: God sent His Son into the world to save our souls, so that we could one day spend eternity with Him. He has spent the better part of 2000 years pleading with the human race to turn back to Him. In light of the big picture of Scripture, we know that "the Lord's primary work is the forgiveness of sins," not the physical healing of our broken, transitory bodies (Richardson, 236).

While it may fully be God's will to heal some physical ailments on this earth, God's ultimate will is to use whatever it takes to turn our eyes to His face, so that we will submit to Him, our glorious Savior.

The last part of verse 15 also seems to raise another troubling question: does sickness mean someone sinned? And again, looking at the whole of Scripture would teach us that this cannot always be true.

In fact, Jesus himself addressed this question in John 9:1-3. Why don't you turn there are read those verses.

If neither the man nor his parents sinned, why, according to Jesus, was the man born blind?

As Richardson notes, "Sin can be an element in the problem of sickness but is not necessarily so" (235). We must be careful not to add to God's Word in areas like this. James nowhere asserts that sickness is caused exclusively by sin, and so we should not come to such conclusions either.

VERSE 16

James has spent the better part of his letter discussing the tongue and its evils. He has also discussed being unmerciful in our judgement of others. And, most recently, he has reminded us not to allow our difficult circumstances to turn us against one another to the point of grumbling against each other.

We think it's safe to say that verse 16 has all of that in mind. James wants to make sure we know that there is a time and place to confess our sins one to another. The purpose of this confession is not to detail every single iota of the sin, but rather to clear the air, so to speak, and ask that brother or sister in Christ to pray with you and for you so that sin isn't committed again.

One of the things James has taught, both directly and indirectly, is that suffering is best endured in the context of community. In fact, we saw that the lack of community and lack of basic life necessities were what made it so difficult for the widows and orphans to endure. We need each other. Isolation is never taught in Scripture; community is. And when we harbor sin against one another, this community is destroyed. Verse 16 is James's cry of warning to fix that rift before it spreads and wreaks more havoc on the family of believers around us.

It is possible that James was referring to something Paul said in Galatians 6:1-2. Paraphrase what Paul said in light of what James is saying here in verse 16. In other words, what about them is similar?

James finishes up this verse with an oft-quoted statement: "The prayer of a righteous person has great power as it is working." James will interject yet another powerful Old Testament example of this statement in the next two verses.

VERSES 17-18

We've talked about Abraham, Rahab, and Job. Now who has James brought to our attention?

The prophet Elijah would have been another well-known person of the faith to these Jews. His story that is recounted here is found in 1 Kings 17. If you don't know his story or need a refresher, feel free to pause to read it now.

James mentioned prophets earlier in chapter 5. He now mentions a specific prophet, Elijah, who had told of a coming drought. This man prayed once that it would not rain and then again that it would rain. And his prayer was powerful and effective, **just** as Jame 5:16b says.

But before James gets too deep into his story about Elijah, what does he tell us about Elijah in the very beginning of verse 17?

You see, James wants us to know from the get-go that Elijah had no special powers. No, Elijah was a simple man **just** like us. His words were not magical. His ways were not magical. What made his prayer work was God's power. When we pray in accordance with God's promises, our prayers will be answered accordingly (Platt, 103). When we find our prayers not being answered, we can most certainly know that what we have asked does not align with God's will. For when our prayers align with His will, our prayers prove to be "powerful and effective" as James says.

Another reason our prayers may not be answered could be attributed to the very point we've revisited already - James 4:3. If our motives are wrong, we can be sure God will not fulfill our request.

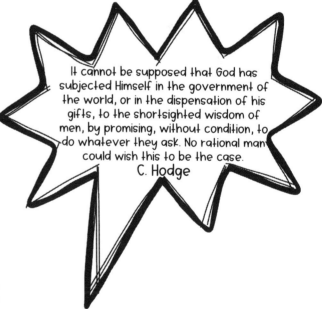

It cannot be supposed that God has subjected Himself in the government of the world, or in the dispensation of his gifts, to the shortsighted wisdom of men, by promising, without condition, to do whatever they ask. No rational man could wish this to be the case.
C. Hodge

What we can take away is this: prayer is vital to our relationship with the Lord. Prayer is beneficial during times of happiness, suffering, injustice, sickness. But prayer is effective only when the answer to our prayer will accomplish God's will. So when we pray, we should "all the while [be] asking Him to change our desires to accord with His will" (Platt, 103).

Why don't we end today doing **just** that. No matter what situation you're dealing with right now - one of suffering, happiness, sickness, injustice - spend some time asking God to change your desires to match His in that particular situation.

DAY 3 >> POWERFUL PRAYER

GOD WHO SEES AND KNOWS ALL,

James began by telling us that he counted himself as a "servant," a slave, "of God and of the Lord Jesus Christ." He has spent 5 chapters - 5 tough-pills-to-swallow chapters - teaching us, commanding us, begging us to keep our eyes on God as we patiently endure what trials we meet along life's way. James has exhorted us to stay close together even though we may be dispersed, as were the Jews in his original audience. He has shown us the power that is found within a community of like-minded believers. But he has also warned us that going astray is incredibly easy, which leads us to his last words in chapter 5.

Go ahead and read James 5:1-20.

Let's head back to chapter 1 for a moment. What did James tell us waaaaay back in chapter 1 verse 14 leads us astray?

It is all too easy to allow our sinful desires to take root again and mislead us. We can be wholeheartedly walking the right way, only to be tempted by our own fleshly desires yet again. And when we are, James says, it is our brothers and sisters around us who should help "bring us back."

If we think back to the brunt of chapter 4, James spent verses 7-10 telling us how to get our hearts back where they should be. He told us that we must submit and repent and draw near to God. But these commands signal that we recognize that we went astray. There are times in our lives where we have wandered from the path we should be on, yet we don't seem to notice. It is then that we need the community of believers around us to take note and lovingly help us get back on track.

Can you think of a time in your life when you have watched someone slip onto a destructive path when that person didn't even realize he or she had changed paths?

When we haven't surrounded ourselves with a godly community of believers, we are at risk for wandering never to return. There is a reason that God calls us to community - and always has - from the very beginning in Genesis. Way back then, we see that God did not say His creation was "very good" until Eve was given to Adam. God knew that they both needed community. As we said yesterday, isolation is never taught in Scripture, but community is.

What about you personally...can you think of a time in your life when you slipped onto a destructive path? Did anyone around you come to your rescue?

James, again, seems to be reiterating what we saw that Paul taught in Galatians 6. Paul was sure to include that when restoration is taking place, it should be done in "gentleness."

Critical thinking for a moment...in light of all that James has taught about sin, our desires, etc., why would gentleness be an important quality when bringing back a wanderer?

James goes on in verse 20 to say that anyone who brings back a wanderer, a sinner, "will save his soul from death." James is in no way implying that the rescuer becomes the savior. James 4:12 would refute that: "There is only one lawgiver and judge, he who is able to save and destroy..."

However, God uses people to accomplish His will. He invites us into His story, His redemptive story. He has given us the job to go into all the world and preach the good news - to make disciples, people who will follow Him. Part of that job is also restoration. As we disciple others, there will be times that it is necessary to bring a wanderer back to the right path. But we must act in gentleness because we have no room to condemn since it is our own sinful desires that draw us away to begin with. We could **just** as easily become the wanderer. And to borrow James's words, if we judge without mercy, no mercy will be shown to us (4:13).

All throughout Scripture, we see that sin destroys our souls. The more we allow sin into our lives, the harder our hearts get toward sin. We become calloused, uncaring. It goes back to what we talked about last week - sin becomes a laughable offense rather than a serious issue when we've allowed ourselves to dive headfirst into it. We need restoration so that our souls are not in danger of this type of death.

James finishes out verse 20 by saying that not only does one who brings back a wanderer "save his soul from death," but also "will cover a multitude of sins."

Look up either Proverbs 10:12 or 1 Peter 4:8. Write one below. Underline the portion of the verse that James's message echoes.

This portion of James 5:20 also shows us the importance of community. "The church is one of the God-ordained means God uses to keep us faithful" (Platt, 104). He allows those around us to point out where we have faltered, so that we can humble ourselves before God, submit to Him, and experience His mercy and compassion, **just** as James has been teaching.

One commentator translated it this way: "love refuses to see faults." He didn't mean that love ignores faults, but rather, once they have been pointed out and dealt with, once the person has confessed the sin to God and has been restored, love no longer points to those faults over and over again. "Love covers a multitude of sins."

LET'S RECAP ▶ ▶▶▶

James has taken us on quite the journey. It hasn't always been smooth sailin' either!

In chapter 1, James...

- ...**beckoned** us to count every trial we meet as joy because in our trials, we are perfected, coming out looking more like Jesus.
- ...**reminded** us that wisdom is ours for the asking.
- ...**warned** us that double-mindedness would land us in trouble every time. The world or Jesus - we have to choose one.
- ...**exposed** the root of our sin: our own desires.
- ...**comforted** us with the knowledge that all good and perfect gifts come straight from our Father - even the gifts that feel a bit painful at first.
- ...**told** us that we should be quick to hear but oh-so-slow to speak or become angry.
- ...**pleaded** with us to be doers, not **just** hearers of God's Words.
- ...**reality-checked** us, reminding us that our religion was worthless if we weren't taking care of widows and orphans.

In chapter 2, James...

- ...**warned** us about showing partiality based on outward appearances.

- ...**reminded** us of the Royal Law - that we should love others as we love ourselves.
- ...**humbled** us by reminding us that we all fall and break the Law.
- ...**exposed** us by teaching us that faith cannot be shown apart from works.

In chapter 3, James...

- **warned** us about becoming teachers because of the stricter judgment that comes with the territory of teaching God's Word.
- **corrected** us about our thinking on the tongue: while it may be small, it's mighty and powerful.
- **informed** us on the difference between heavenly wisdom and worldly wisdom.

In chapter 4, James...

- ...**called** us out for our quarrels and fights, only to reveal the issue is our heart - our selfish, murderous, adulterous hearts.
- ...**taught** us how to repent and turn back to God so that we might find forgiveness and restoration.
- ...**reminded** us that God is the only Judge.
- ...**cautioned** us about the short breadth of life on this earth.

In chapter 5, James...

- ...**warned** the rich that their time to repent was short and almost gone.
- ...**exemplified** patience in visible ways that we might remember his message: patiently endure.
- ...**reminded** us of the power of prayer and the purpose of prayer.
- ...**emphasized** the necessity of community.

In all of this, James had one goal in mind. He wanted to do precisely what he **just** closed his letter by saying. He wanted to bring those Jews who had wandered from the truth back to the way of God's Light. He wanted to restore them. He wanted to remind them that God has a purpose for every trial. He wanted them to know that God redeems even the greatest injustice. He wanted them to understand that they still had time to turn back to Him, submit to Him, serve Him.

And wouldn't he say the same to us? Isn't his message for us, too? We don't know where the end of this study finds you, but we can be sure that you can find yourself somewhere between chapter 1 and chapter 5. Whether you are in the midst of a trial, suffering an injustice, wandering from God's way, struggling with your tongue, needing prayer, desperate for community...James's message is for you.

His goal - and ours, too - would be for you to be able to proclaim boldly in the middle of whatever circumstance is staring you down right now that you are a **#justteacher** who's living a **#justlife #justlikeJames** and **#justlikeJesus**.

Story Time: When I travel, I tend to pack **#allthethings** because one should have **#alltheoptions.** Am I right!?!? My suitcase is full, and everything is packed neatly inside to ensure that **#allthethings** will fit. Problems ensue when I have to make the return trek back home because **#allthethings** that I packed no longer fit. No matter how hard I try, my suitcase is always bursting at the seams. The puzzle pieces don't fit so neatly anymore. The extra space zipper on my suitcase is always used to accommodate everything that is crammed inside my bag.

When we began our journey through the book of James, I knew that our suitcases would be full of information. In fact, in my past reading and studying of the book of James, everything fit nicely in a fully-packed suitcase. However, now that we are at the end of our journey, the suitcase that I packed ever so neatly, is now bursting at the seams. The harsh truths found in James are quite literally overflowing out of my spiritual suitcase. James kept pointing me back to my main issue - my heart. I don't know about you, but often in my life, I treat the symptom and not the problem. James reminded us that our main problem was our heart.

> "Keep your heart with all vigilance, for from it flow the springs of life." Proverbs 4:23

Throughout the course of writing this study with Bethany, I went through an extremely difficult trial. It was heart-wrenching. I felt weak and broken. In those moments of weakness, I ran to Jesus and the book of James. James's words were blunt, bold, and truthful. Yet in the midst of his bluntness, I found peace and healing. In every second of my pain, God proved Himself faithful and **just**. James reminded me that my pain was not meaningless and because of that pain, I love Jesus even more. As I preached the truth of His Word to my own heart and mind, I found that my pain turned to singing of His glory and His goodness.

This was not my first trial, and it certainly won't be my last. I don't know where you are right now in your life. Are you on the heels of a trial, in the midst of a trial, or on the other side of one? Trials come in various sizes, shapes, and forms, and each trial has a purpose. We may not ever truly understand the purpose of trials that we walk through in our lives, but one thing is for certain - our goal is to love Jesus more in the middle of storm so that we may stand stronger on the other side of the storm.

How is this accomplished?

Around these parts - we love a good storm. We mean a literal storm. This past school year, we ended up with more hurricane days than snow days. I think what we love is the adventure of preparing for the upcoming storm that may or may not keep us out of school for a couple of days. One particular snow storm prep stands out in my mind: we were expecting 6 to 10 inches of snow in our area. Everyone was in prep mode. **#northernersdontjudgeus** We knew that we might lose power and be out of school for several days. Bethany decided to come stay in my home for the duration - we often use those times for writing. While we knew that the storm was coming, we didn't take our prep seriously until the night before. We found ourselves in the middle of Walmart with no bread, no water, no snacks. I am the queen of eating out, and my shelves at home were quite bare. We had to get creative so that we would be able to have food over the course of the next few days.

Bethany and I had a problem: we waited until the very last moment to prepare for the impending storm. Y'all! Doesn't that sound like what we do when spiritual storms hit? We scramble to prepare for what is about to hit us or, worse, we wait until we suddenly find ourselves in the middle of the trial. Dear teacher friend, don't scramble. James would tell you to prepare for the storm by day by day by preaching the truths of God's Word to your heart and mind. Those truths will become peace in the midst of your storms when you **#justrelyonJesus.** He brings peace that passes all human understanding that allows us to find songs in the night (Psalm 77:6). In those trial-filled moments, we will begin to unpack our overstuffed spiritual suitcase, and what we thought was excessive and overstuffed will become **#justwhatweneed.**

Stuff your suitcase with Truth...

**THOUGHT YOU SLAY ME
SHANE & SHANE FEATURING JOHN PIPER**
http://bit.ly/JustJamesThoughYouSlayMe

Bonnie Kathryn

James has always been one of my favorite books. I've read it through more times than I can count. But I can honestly say that I've never plumbed its depths like we have the last 6 weeks. Truths were revealed that I have never before connected. I can only attribute that to the Author of this Holy Book. When He knows our hearts are ready, He sows the seed, waters it, makes it grow, and then reaps the harvest at **just** the right time.

When I think of James, I feel like it all hinges on his opening verses: "Count it all joy, my brothers, when you face trials of various kinds, knowing that the testing of your faith produces patience. But let patience have its perfect work, that you may be perfect and complete, lacking nothing."

Joy in the midst of trials is never easy, but I can say boldly from experience, there is joy to be found in the darkness.

Jeremiah was a prophet who experienced much heartache and hardship because of the message that God gave him to pass on to the people of Israel. His words have been branded on my heart for some years now: "Your words were found, and I devoured them, and they were to me the joy and rejoicing of my heart" (15:16). What Jeremiah proclaimed is exactly what James taught: in the midst of trials, we are meant to press into God and His Word. We are meant to devour them hungrily - all of them…the words of lament, the words of praise, the words of mourning, the words of trust…all of them - and when we begin to digest them, they become to our hearts joy and rejoicing because they teach us, they remind us, they encourage us to remember that God is good…and only good.

What I've learned over the years is that when I let God use a trial in the way He desires - to accomplish in me and through me whatever it is He wills - then it does indeed perfect me and make me more like Him. But when I fight Him in the midst of a trial, I also have seen that the type of trial repeats itself because He's after something…He's after perfecting me, He's after molding me because He wants me to mirror Him more clearly.

I don't want to fight Him. I want His will. I want His way. I want whatever it takes that is going to make me more like Him. I want whatever is going to make me look up at Him.

Am I going to stumble along the way? Sure. Is my tongue going to get me in trouble at times…too many times? Absolutely. But will there be forgiveness and mercy and restoration? You bet… because "He gives more grace."

I'm not sure where you are right now, what your life looks like, what trials you may be facing, but what I do know is that if you will do as Jeremiah did…

- if you will search for His Words - they can't be found if you don't search for them,
- if you will devour them - no baby bites, big large gulps…your heart is starving for His Word,

…you WILL find that they become the joy and rejoicing of your heart. Your heart will sense that your God is FOR you, never against you - no matter how much the look of your circumstances tries to betray that truth. He is for you. And He is good. ONLY good. **#justgood**

So count it all joy, my friends…until next time… *Bethany*

"Blue Letter Bible." *Blue Letter Bible*, www.blueletterbible.org/.

"Matthew Henry Complete Bible Commentary Online." *Bible Study Tools*, www.biblestudytools.com/commentaries/matthew-henry-complete/.

McGiffert, Arthur. *The Church History of Eusebius*. Messes, Parker, and Co., 1890. *Google Books*. https://play.google.com/books/reader?id=PG07AQAAMAAJ&hl=en&pg=GBS.PP11

Patrick, Charles. "Modern Day Molech." *Southwestern Baptist Theological Seminary*, swbts.edu/news/releases/modern-day-molech/.

Platt, David, et al. *Exalting Jesus in James*. Holman Reference, 2014.

Richardson, Kurt A. *James*. Broadman & Holman, 1997.

"Robertson's Word Pictures of the New Testament Bible Commentary." *Bible Study Tools*, www.biblestudytools.com/commentaries/robertsons-word-pictures/.

Wilkin, Jen. *Women of the Word: How to Study the Bible with Both Our Hearts and Our Minds*. Crossway Books, 2019.

Author Credits:
Bethany Fleming
Bonnie Hunter

TEACHERS IN THE *Word*
a ministry of
BONNIE KATHRYN TEACHING

Made in the USA
Lexington, KY
06 June 2019